Pathfinder

A Beginner's Guide to Hiking Success

MOWSER

Copyright © 2025 by Mowser

All rights reserved. No part of this book may be used or reproduced in any form whatsoever without written permission except in the case of brief quotations in critical articles or reviews.

This ebook may contain links to affiliate websites and we may receive an affiliate commission for any purchases made by you on the affiliate website using such links.

For more information, or to book an event, contact :
mowser@mowser.com.au
http://www.mowser.com.au

Book design by Mowser
Cover design by Mowser

All chapter icons from Flaticon:
https://www.flaticon.com

ISBN - Ebook: 9781763873803
ISBN - Paperback: 9781763873810

First Edition: January 2025

Disclaimer

The information in this book is intended for general educational and informational purposes only. It is not a substitute for professional advice, instruction, or guidance specific to your individual circumstances. Hiking, trekking, bushwalking and other outdoor activities involve inherent risks, and readers are encouraged to assess their personal fitness levels, experience, and the conditions of the trails they choose before undertaking any activity described in this book.

The author and publisher are not responsible for any injuries, damages, or losses resulting from the use or misuse of the information provided. Readers are advised to research and prepare adequately for any hiking or outdoor activity, including consulting local regulations, weather conditions, and safety guidelines. Always use your own judgment and exercise caution.

By continuing to read and apply the content of this book, you acknowledge that you accept full responsibility for your actions and decisions.

CONTENTS

THE TRANSFORMATIVE POWER OF HIKING 2

WHY I'M QUALIFIED TO GUIDE YOU 5

WHY HIKE? 8

UNDERSTANDING TRACKS AND TRAILS FOR YOUR FIRST WALK 14

ESSENTIAL HIKING GEAR 28
    Weather-Related Gear Guide 35
    Quick-Reference Day Hike Checklist 44

NAVIGATION FOR BEGINNERS 47

PLANNING YOUR FIRST HIKE 58

FOOD AND HYDRATION ON THE TRAIL 66

SAFETY ESSENTIALS 76
    Emergency Shelter & Fire Starting Essentials 79
    Tips for Quick Deployment 80

HOW TO STAY COMFORTABLE OUTDOORS 87

SETTING UP FOR SUCCESS ON OVERNIGHT HIKES 95
    Quick-Reference Overnight Hiking Checklist 104

PROBLEM-SOLVING ON THE TRAIL 107
    QUICK-REFERENCE GUIDE FOR COMMON TRAIL PROBLEMS 112

LEARNING FROM MISTAKES	117
BUILDING YOUR CONFIDENCE AND SKILLS	126
ECO-FRIENDLY HIKING	132
WHAT'S NEXT? LEVELLING UP YOUR HIKING ADVENTURES	140
ABOUT THE AUTHOR	149

INTRODUCTION

The Transformative Power of Hiking

Hiking isn't just about putting one foot in front of the other. It's about stepping out of your comfort zone and into a world where every track or trail tells a story, and every summit unveils a new perspective.

Whether it's a short walk through a local forest or an adventurous climb to a hilltop lookout, hiking has an unparalleled ability to refresh the mind, invigorate the body, and awaken the spirit.

For beginners however, the world of hiking can feel overwhelming. What gear should you bring? How do you pick the right trail? What if something goes wrong? These questions often stop people before they even lace up their boots. That's why this guide exists: to take the guesswork out of hiking and give you the confidence to step onto the trail with excitement rather than hesitation.

Who This Guide Is For ?

This guide is tailored for those who are ready to embrace the outdoors but might not know where to start.

Perhaps you've admired hikers on social media and wondered if you could do the same. Maybe a friend or family member has invited you on a hike, and you want to be prepared. Or perhaps you're looking for a way to disconnect from the rush of daily life and reconnect with nature. Whatever your reason, this guide is designed to meet you where you are, with no prior hiking experience required. You don't need to be an athlete or a wilderness expert to enjoy hiking. With a bit of preparation and the right mindset, anyone can experience the joys of hiking.

The First Steps Towards Confidence

At its core, hiking is simple. But simplicity doesn't mean there's nothing to learn. The difference between a delightful day on the trail and a frustrating or even dangerous experience often comes down to preparation.

That's why this guide doesn't just tell you what to do—it explains why each step is important, so you can make informed decisions every time you hike.

From choosing the right gear to giving you a basic understanding of maps and weather, this guide equips you with foundational knowledge that will make your hikes safer, more comfortable, and more enjoyable.

By focusing on day hikes and single overnighters, we'll help you master the basics without the added complexities of multi-day expeditions.

A Journey, Not Just a Destination

One of the most beautiful aspects of hiking is that it's a deeply personal journey. Your first hike might be a gentle stroll along a riverside, while your future hikes could take you to alpine peaks or remote beaches. Regardless of where you start or how far you go, hiking offers a sense of accomplishment and connection that few activities can match.

This guide is more than a collection of tips and tricks—it's a companion on your first steps into the world of hiking. Together, we'll build your skills, grow your confidence, and help you discover the magic of the outdoors. By the end, you won't just feel prepared—you'll feel inspired to keep exploring, one trail at a time.

PROLOGUE

Why I'm Qualified to Guide You

Hiking has been a defining part of my life for over 30 years. I've spent countless days—and nights, adding up to months and years—on the trails, navigating everything from serene forest paths to rugged mountain landscapes. My love for the outdoors started small, with short family day walks as a child and a cub/scout and has since grown into a lifelong passion that has taken me to some of the most breathtaking and remote locations imaginable, including the pristine wilderness of Tasmania, where I've spent years exploring and learning its unique challenges.

Over the decades, I've experienced nearly every aspect of hiking: the exhilaration of reaching a summit, the fear of dealing with unexpected events, the solitude of remote tracks, and yes, even the frustrations and mistakes that come with stepping into the unknown trackless regions of my home state.

These experiences—both the highs and the lessons learned the hard way—are what I bring to this guide. I know what it's like to be a beginner, nervously stepping onto a trail for the first time, unsure of what to pack, how to stay safe, or even how to find the right path. And I know the immense satisfaction of overcoming those uncertainties and growing into a confident, capable hiker.

My journey as a hiker hasn't just been about walking bush tracks; it's been about observing, experimenting, and refining. Over the years, I've developed a deep understanding of the strategies, gear, and mindset needed to make every hike a success. From navigating Tasmanian rainforests and peaks where weather can change in minutes to finding ways to keep morale high during challenging weeklong trips, I've learned what works—and what doesn't—through firsthand experience.

Beyond personal experience, I've dedicated time to sharing my knowledge with others. Having worked as a professional guide on Tasmania's Overland Track, I've guided clients, friends, family, and beginner hikers, helping them build confidence and find joy in the outdoors.

In addition to guiding clients and friends, I've also grown a YouTube channel and newsletter to a large following, inspiring others to develop confidence on the trail, make informed gear choices, and embrace the adventure of the outdoors.

Watching someone go from hesitant to hooked on hiking is one of the most rewarding experiences, and it's inspired me to create this guide. I understand the questions, concerns, and challenges beginners face because I've helped countless people navigate them.

Living in Tasmania has given me a unique perspective as well. The terrain here is as beautiful as it is challenging, offering lessons in resilience, adaptability, and preparation. Whether it's dealing with sudden rain squalls, navigating through dense vegetation, or camping in remote locations, Tasmania's wilderness has taught me that hiking isn't just about reaching the destination—it's about how you prepare, adapt, and grow along the way.

I've written this guide not as an expert speaking down to beginners, but as someone who remembers what it's like to be in your shoes. I've been there, and I've made the mistakes, so you don't have to. This book is my way of sharing decades of lessons, tips, and insights to help you start your hiking journey with confidence. Whether you're planning your first day hike or dreaming of an overnight adventure, I'm here to guide you every step of the way.

So, let's get started—your adventure awaits!

Mowser

January 2025

CHAPTER 1

Why Hike?

Hiking is so much more than just walking in nature—it's a doorway to experiences that enrich the body, mind, and spirit. Unlike a stroll through the neighbourhood or a run on a treadmill, hiking immerses you in the rhythms of the natural world. Each track or trail is unique, offering new challenges, discoveries, and moments of connection. It's an activity that allows you to step away from the demands of daily life and into a space where you can breathe deeply, move freely, and simply be present.

Whether you're drawn to the quiet beauty of a forest or the awe-inspiring vistas of a mountain range, hiking has something to offer everyone.

THE PHYSICAL HEALTH BENEFITS OF HIKING

The physical benefits of hiking are well-documented. It's a dynamic form of exercise that strengthens your muscles, improves cardiovascular health, and boosts endurance—all while being gentler on your joints compared to high-impact sports. Climbing hills and navigating uneven trails engages your legs and core, while carrying a backpack adds resistance that tones your upper body. Hiking also burns calories effectively, helping you manage your weight without feeling like a chore. What's more, the variety of movements involved keeps your body adaptable and resilient. You're not just exercising—you're building the strength and stamina to face life's physical challenges with greater ease.

Mental Clarity and Reduced Stress

But the benefits of hiking aren't confined to the body; they extend deeply into the mind. Stepping into nature has a proven ability to reduce stress and promote mental clarity. The gentle rhythm of walking, combined with the soothing sights and sounds of the outdoors, creates a meditative effect that calms racing thoughts and eases anxiety. Time on the trail becomes a digital detox, giving your brain a break from the constant notifications and distractions of modern life. This mental respite can leave you feeling refreshed, focused, and more creative when you return to your daily routine.

The Mindfulness Connection

Hiking also fosters mindfulness, inviting you to be fully present in the moment. It's hard to worry about tomorrow's deadlines when you're captivated by the sound of a nearby stream or the way sunlight filters through the trees. The trail demands your attention—each step requires focus, especially on uneven terrain, pulling you into the here and now.

This practice of mindfulness, whether intentional or spontaneous, can transform your perspective. It reminds you to appreciate life's simple pleasures and find joy in the small, often-overlooked details of the world around you.

Reconnecting With Nature

One of the most profound aspects of hiking is its ability to reconnect us with nature. In a world where many of us spend our days indoors, the chance to immerse ourselves in the natural environment can feel almost revolutionary.

Hiking puts you face-to-face with the beauty and diversity of the earth. From the sound of wind over a ridgetop to the sight of wildlife, nature stimulates the senses and fills us with a sense of wonder. This connection isn't just uplifting—it's also deeply restorative.

Building Resilience and Confidence

Hiking is a journey of resilience. Trails often present obstacles, such as steep inclines or unpredictable weather, and overcoming these builds both physical and mental strength. With each challenge conquered—whether it's reaching a peak or navigating rocky terrain—you grow more confident in your abilities. This resilience transfers to everyday life, giving you the tools to face challenges with greater self-assurance. For beginners, starting with easier trails and progressively tackling more difficult ones can be a rewarding way to develop this skill without feeling overwhelmed.

Discovering Holistic Growth Through the Art of Hiking

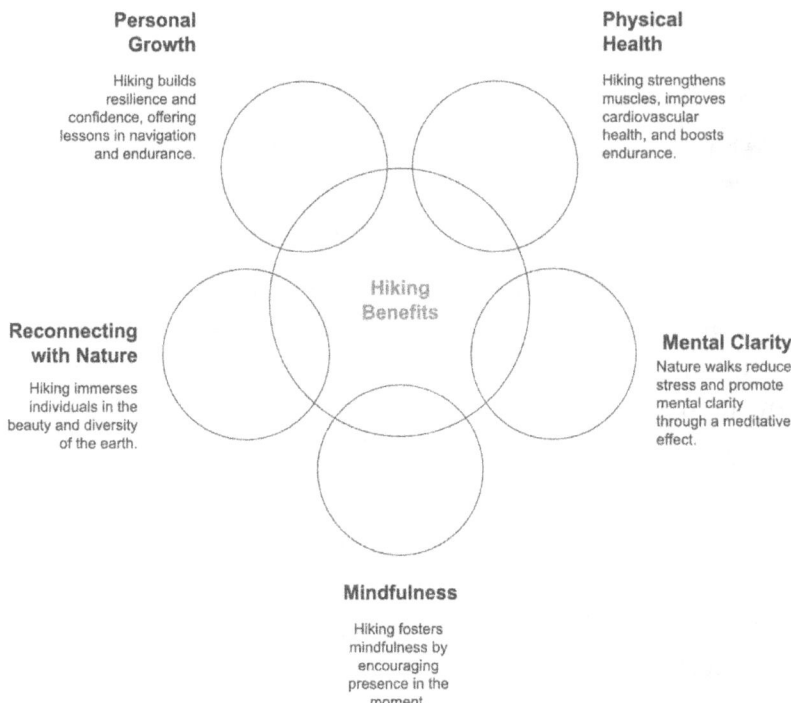

FOSTERING SOCIAL CONNECTIONS

While hiking can be a solitary experience, it's also a fantastic way to connect with others. Sharing the trail with friends or family creates opportunities for bonding and meaningful conversations. Even joining a local hiking group can introduce you to a community of like-minded individuals who share your love for the outdoors. Walking side by side encourages open communication, fostering relationships that are strengthened by shared experiences, from moments of laughter to overcoming challenges together.

A Sustainable and Accessible Adventure

Hiking is one of the most sustainable and accessible outdoor activities. It doesn't require expensive equipment or memberships—just a good pair of shoes and a sense of adventure. Trails exist in most areas, from city parks to remote wilderness, making hiking accessible to a wide range of people. By practising Leave No Trace principles, you can enjoy these natural spaces responsibly, ensuring that they remain beautiful for generations to come. Hiking is an eco-friendly way to enjoy the planet while cultivating a sense of stewardship for its future.

Personal Growth Through Hiking

Hiking is also a pathway to personal growth. Each trail teaches you something new, whether it's about navigation, endurance, or simply how to pack smarter. As you tackle different challenges, you develop problem-solving skills and gain a deeper understanding of your strengths and limits. These lessons extend beyond the trail, influencing how you approach challenges in other areas of your life. Hiking becomes more than a physical journey—it's a journey of self-discovery.

A Life Long Adventure

Perhaps the most beautiful thing about hiking is its longevity as an activity. Whether you're a young adult exploring the outdoors for the first time or a retiree revisiting favourite trails, hiking can be tailored to your needs and interests. Every season brings new opportunities to experience the landscape in a different way, from the vibrant greens of spring to the crisp air of autumn. With an ever- growing list of trails to explore, hiking becomes a lifelong adventure that evolves alongside you, providing endless opportunities for joy, growth, and connection.

> **KEY TAKEAWAYS**
>
> - Hiking is more than just walking—it's an immersive experience that strengthens the body, clears the mind, and deepens your connection with nature.
> - It offers significant physical benefits, improving cardiovascular health, endurance, and muscle strength while being low-impact on joints.
> - Time on the trail reduces stress, enhances focus, and provides a much-needed break from digital distractions.
> - Overcoming obstacles on the trail builds resilience and confidence, skills that carry over into everyday life.
> - Hiking can be a solo journey of self-reflection or a shared experience that strengthens friendships and builds community.
> - It's one of the most accessible and sustainable outdoor activities, requiring minimal gear and offering lifelong adventure.
> - Every hike presents an opportunity for personal growth, teaching valuable lessons in problem-solving, adaptability, and perseverance.

CHAPTER 2

UNDERSTANDING TRACKS AND TRAILS FOR YOUR FIRST WALK

THE IMPORTANCE OF CHOOSING THE RIGHT TRAIL

When you're just starting out, selecting the right track or trail can make or break your first hiking experience. Too difficult, and you may find yourself overwhelmed or wore yet - injured. Too easy, and it might feel underwhelming, leaving you wondering what all the fuss is about. The perfect trail strikes a balance between being challenging enough to feel rewarding while still matching your fitness levels and goals. Picking the right trail is about knowing yourself, your abilities, and what kind of experience you're looking for.

Choosing the Perfect Hiking Trail

Assess Fitness   Identify Goals   Evaluate Trails   Select Trail

What Makes a Trail Beginner-Friendly?

Beginner-friendly trails have a few common characteristics: they're relatively short, have gentle inclines, and are well-marked. Trails like these allow you to get a feel for hiking

without overexerting yourself or risking getting lost. Pay attention to factors like distance, elevation gain, and the trail surface. For instance, a trail with minimal rocky or uneven sections will be easier to navigate than one requiring technical skills. These factors are usually listed on visitor information maps or descriptions online, making them a good starting point for your research.

Understanding Trail Ratings and Difficulty Levels

Most trails are categorised by difficulty: easy, moderate, and difficult.

- Easy trails are typically shorter, with minimal elevation gain and a well-maintained surface.

- Moderate trails might involve steeper climbs or longer distances.

- Difficult trails can include rocky terrain, significant elevation changes, and even exposure to high altitudes.

As a beginner, stick to easy or moderate trails that fit within your fitness level and experience. This ensures a positive experience without overdoing it. And just remember that for the purposes of this book, we are primarily talking about day walks and to some extent, overnight hikes. We'll cover extended trips in a future book!

Which trail difficulty should I choose?

Easy Trails

Suitable for beginners with minimal elevation and short distances, ensuring a positive experience.

Moderate Trails

For those with some experience, involving steeper climbs or longer distances.

Difficult Trails

Best for experienced hikers, featuring rocky terrain and significant elevation changes.

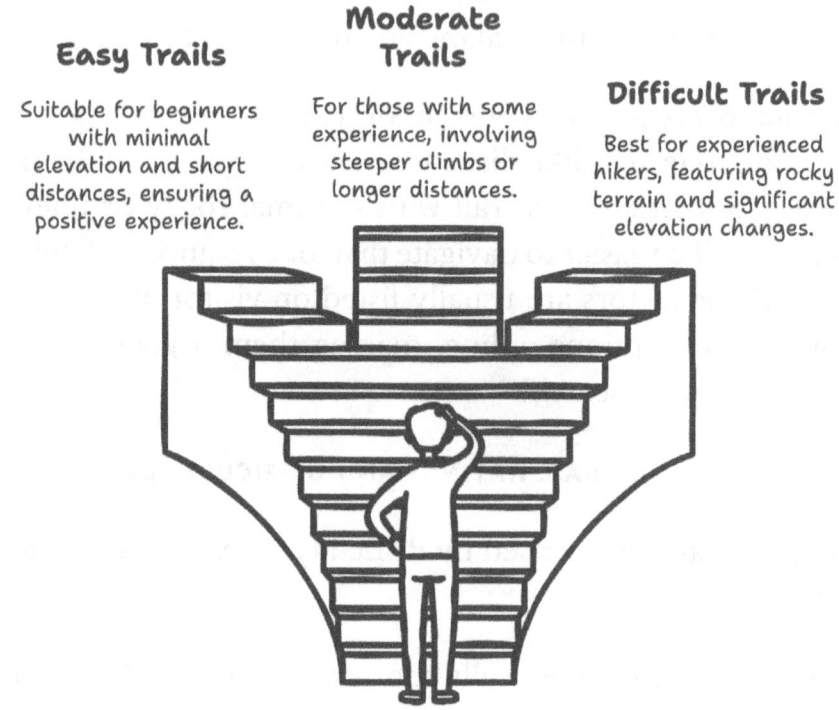

THE ROLE OF ELEVATION GAIN

Elevation gain refers to the total amount of climbing you'll do on a trail. It's a crucial factor when assessing a hike's difficulty. A trail that gains 100 metres (328 feet) over 5 kilometres (3.1 miles) is a lot gentler than one gaining the same 100 metres over 1 kilometre. If you're new to hiking, look for trails with less than 300 metres of elevation gain for the duration of the walk. This will allow you to focus on enjoying the hike without being overly taxed by steep climbs.

Trail Length: How Much Can You Handle?

Beginners, and even experienced hikers, often underestimate the time and energy required to complete a walk. A good rule of thumb is to start with hikes that are 3 to 5 kilometres long (1.9-3.1 miles). This distance gives you enough time to enjoy the trail without pushing your limits. As you gain experience and stamina, you can gradually increase the distance. Remember to account for breaks, photos, and time spent enjoying the scenery when estimating how long a trail will take. Many people can overlook this factor when planning their first walks.

Weather Conditions and Seasonal Factors

The time of year and current weather conditions play a significant role in trail selection. In summer, trails at lower elevations can be hot and dry, making higher-elevation routes more appealing.

Conversely, winter hikes may require extra preparation, such as warm clothing or snow gear. Some trails can become muddy or icy during certain seasons, increasing the risk of slips and falls.

I have experienced this firsthand having broken my leg on a winter trip in somewhat deceiving conditions–a sunny, yet frosty Tasmanian winters day! Always check the weather forecast and trail conditions before heading out and choose a trail that aligns with the conditions.

Trail Markers and Navigation

One of the most reassuring aspects of beginner trails is the presence of clear trail markers. Depending upon what part of the world you are in, these signs or markers can vary greatly. In Tasmania and Australia, they are typically indicated by orange triangular trail markers. But they can also include the following.

- Markings painted on trees, rocks, or posts and help guide you along the path.

- Cairns (known in some places as ducks) are piles of rocks and can be found in areas where other marking options are difficult. E.g. on alpine ridgetops or rocky ridgelines. These can be very large piles (on summits) or smaller piles giving a track line.

- Tapes tied to trees and vegetation. These can be a variety of different colours. In Tasmania, often, they tend to be pink.

Before setting out, familiarise yourself with these markers and the trail's map and any key landmarks. Apps like AllTrails or Gaia GPS can also be invaluable for navigation, but it's wise to carry a physical map as a backup in case your phone battery dies, or you lose signal.

Finding Trail Information Online

The internet is a treasure trove of trail information. Websites such as AllTrails, Gaia GPS, and local national parks official pages provide detailed descriptions of trails, including difficulty ratings, distance, elevation gain, and user reviews. These platforms often include photos and tips from other hikers, giving you a clearer picture of what to expect. Reading reviews can help you anticipate challenges, such as muddy sections or confusing junctions, and make a more informed decision.

Social media and online hiking groups can also be valuable sources of information, with many communities dedicated to specific tracks and regions. However, be wary—some online posts may be outdated, biased, or inaccurate. Trail conditions change, and personal opinions vary widely. Always cross-reference information from multiple sources, including guidebooks, national park websites, and reputable hiking platforms, to ensure you're getting the most accurate and up-to-date details before heading out.

Local Parks and Nature Reserves

For your first hikes, consider trails within local parks or nature reserves. These areas often have well-maintained paths and plenty of signage, making them ideal for beginners. Additionally, they're usually close to amenities like parking, and visitor centres, which can be comforting if you're new to hiking. Starting close to home also reduces the pressure of a long drive before or after your hike. Even where I live in Tasmania, there are many walking trails within a short drive of the urban centres. You certainly don't have to travel far to find a good trail to start out on!

Apps and Technology for Trail Selection

Smartphone apps have revolutionised how we find and plan hikes. Apps like [AllTrails](), [Gaia GPS](), and many more allow you to filter trails by length, difficulty, and user ratings. Some apps even provide downloadable maps for offline use, which can be a lifesaver if you're in an area with poor reception.

However, while these tools are incredibly helpful, always cross-check the information with official sources to ensure accuracy. Never rely on one source alone. Cross check against at least two sources to ensure you are receiving the correct information.

Hiking with a Purpose

Think about what you want from your hike. Are you looking for stunning views, a peaceful forest walk, or a chance to see wildlife? Trails often have unique features, such as waterfalls, lookouts, or historic sites, that can make your experience more memorable. Knowing your purpose helps narrow down your options and ensures you choose a trail that matches your interests.

Understanding Loop, Out-and-Back, and Point-to-Point Trails

Trails come in various formats, each offering a different experience.

- Loop trails start and end at the same point, giving you new scenery throughout.
- Out-and-back trails involve retracing your steps, which can be easier for navigation.
- Point- to-point trails require transportation at both ends, which might complicate logistics.

For beginners, loop or out-and- back trails are often the simplest and most enjoyable options to get started with.

The Role of Trail Amenities

Amenities like bathrooms, picnic areas, and water sources can make a big difference on your first hike. Trails within national parks or popular urban hiking areas are more likely to have these facilities. Check trail descriptions for information about amenities and plan your hike accordingly. Even small comforts, like a shaded rest area, can make your experience more enjoyable if it's your first trip.

Wildlife and Safety Considerations

Understanding the local wildlife is crucial when choosing a trail. Here in Australia, some areas may have snakes, or other potentially dangerous animals, while others are relatively free of threats. If you're in the USA, then bears need to be considered. Always research what to expect and follow recommended safety guidelines, such as knowing what to do if bitten by a snake, carrying bear spray or avoiding feeding animals. Being prepared can help you feel more confident on the trail.

Accessibility and Logistics

Accessibility is another important factor. How far is the start of the walk from where you live? Is there parking, and is it free? Do you need a parks pass? Are dogs allowed if you want to bring a furry companion? These practical considerations might seem minor but can greatly impact your overall experience. Opt for trails that are easy to access and have clear information about their rules and regulations.

Starting Small and Scaling Up

When planning your first hike, it's better to underestimate your abilities than to overestimate them. Trust me. Choose a trail that feels almost too easy and use it as a baseline. If you finish feeling energised and ready for more, you can gradually take on longer and more challenging hikes. This approach helps you build confidence and ensures you don't end up overwhelmed on your first outing.

Hiking Alone vs. With Others

Decide whether you want to hike alone or with a group. Solo hiking offers solitude and a chance to connect deeply with nature but requires more confidence and preparation. Hiking with others, especially experienced hikers, can provide a sense of security and shared enjoyment. Plus, you'll probably also learn more at the same time! If you're unsure, joining a local hiking club or asking a friend to accompany you can be a great way to start.

Safety Tip: Hike Smart, Hike Safe
If you're new to hiking, it's best to hike with a group or an experienced partner until you build confidence and essential skills. Solo hiking requires advanced preparation, strong navigation skills, and the ability to handle unexpected situations alone. Always let someone know your planned route and expected return time before heading out.

Preparing for the Unexpected

Even on beginner-friendly trails, it's important to prepare for the unexpected. Carry essentials like water, snacks, a first-aid kit, and a map. Even if it's just a two-hour stroll in the wilderness.

If you're hiking in cooler weather, bring an extra layer of clothing. Let someone know your plans and expected return time, especially if the trail is in a remote area. These small precautions can make a big difference in ensuring your safety. You can use your trip planner included with this book to plan your walk. Then email it or print it out and leave it with someone so that they know your plans. You can also download the planner at this link.

KNOWING WHEN TO CALL IT OFF

One of the most important lessons for any hiker—beginner or experienced—is understanding when it's time to cancel or turn back. While it can feel disappointing to abandon plans, prioritising safety is always the right choice. If weather conditions worsen or an injury arises before or during the hike, don't hesitate to reassess. Pushing forward despite clear red flags can turn a simple hike into a dangerous situation.

For instance, if the forecast predicts severe storms, high winds, or extreme heat, it's better to postpone your hike rather than risk discomfort or harm. Similarly, if you're feeling unwell or dealing with a nagging injury, hiking could worsen your condition. A trail will still be there tomorrow, but pushing your limits in unsafe conditions could lead to consequences that derail your hiking journey entirely.

The best hikers know that cancelling or turning back isn't a failure—it's a sign of good judgment. It's about making choices that keep you safe and allow you to enjoy hiking for years to come. Always remember: the outdoors is an ever-present invitation. There will always be another day to hike.

> As I write, this I have just had to cancel a six-day family walk due to an ankle injury I sustained... on another walk. It's gut wrenching and disappointing but I know it's the right decision. We'll try again soon but for now, my ankle is thanking me.

Beginner Hiking Success

Personal Goals
Define what you want from the hike

Planning Tools
Use apps and websites for trail information

Difficulty Levels
Easy, moderate, and difficult trail categories

Trail Characteristics
Short, gentle, well-marked, and easy to navigate

Trail Selection
Choose trails matching fitness and goals

Setting Realistic Expectations

Your first hike is unlikely to be perfect, and that's okay. You might take longer than expected, get a little disoriented, or realise that you packed too much. These experiences are part of the learning curve and help you grow as a hiker. By setting realistic expectations and approaching your first hike with curiosity and a sense of adventure, you're setting yourself up for a rewarding experience.

Reflecting on Your Experience

After your hike, take some time to reflect. What did you enjoy most? What would you do differently next time? Every hike is an opportunity to learn more about your preferences, strengths, and areas for improvement. By reflecting on your experience, you can refine your approach and look forward to your next adventure with even greater enthusiasm.

All of this equips you with everything you need to select and prepare for your first hike. With the right trail and mindset, you'll lay the foundation for a lifelong love of hiking.

Key Takeaways

- Choosing the right trail is essential for a positive experience—too difficult can lead to exhaustion or injury, too easy might feel underwhelming.
- Beginner-friendly trails are well-marked, relatively short, and have gentle inclines to help build confidence without unnecessary risk.
- Understanding trail ratings, elevation gain, and distance ensures you pick a route suited to your fitness level and hiking goals.
- Seasonal changes impact trail conditions—always check weather forecasts and be prepared for elements like heat, cold, or unexpected storms.
- Navigation is key—familiarise yourself with trail markers, carry a map, and use apps like AllTrails or Gaia GPS while keeping a backup plan.
- Researching trails using multiple sources (official park websites, hiking apps, guidebooks) ensures accurate and up-to-date information.
- Amenities, accessibility, and logistics—like transport, parking, and required permits—should be considered before heading out.
- Start small and gradually increase difficulty as you gain experience. A well-planned hike leads to a safer, more enjoyable adventure.

CHAPTER 3

Essential Hiking Gear

WHY THE RIGHT GEAR MATTERS

Having the right gear is crucial for a safe, comfortable, and an enjoyable hiking experience. It doesn't mean you need to spend a fortune on the latest gadgets, but investing in reliable essentials can make all the difference.

The right gear ensures you're prepared for the trail ahead; it helps you handle unexpected situations and enhances your overall enjoyment. This chapter breaks down the key gear every beginner hiker needs and explains how to choose items that fit your budget and needs.

> And a note: We are just talking about shorter day walk trips here. We'll go into tents, sleeping bags and all manner of other gear in a future book!

Footwear: The Foundation of Every Hike

Your footwear is arguably the most critical piece of hiking gear. A good pair of hiking boots or shoes provides the support, traction, and protection you need on varied terrain.

Choose footwear based on the type of trails you'll be tackling—lightweight trail runners may suffice for well-groomed paths, while rugged boots are better for rocky or uneven trails.

Pay attention to fit: your toes should have enough room to wiggle, and your heels shouldn't slip. Always break in your footwear before a hike to prevent blisters and discomfort. I always recommend trying on your footwear before buying.

Local hiking shops are a great resource for advice so ensure you take your time in deciding on the best fit for your feet.

Socks: The Unsung Heroes

Many beginner hikers underestimate the importance of good hiking socks. Cotton socks should be avoided at all costs because they retain moisture, which can lead to blisters. Instead, opt for moisture-wicking materials like merino wool or synthetic blends. These socks keep your feet dry, regulate temperature, and provide cushioning where it's needed most.

Investing in quality socks is a small cost for significant comfort. I personally love [Silverlight socks](#) but there are a wide variety of brands available so do your research and find what works for you.

Backpacks: Carrying the Essentials

Your backpack is your mobile storage unit, carrying everything you need for the trail. For day hikes, a 15-30 litre backpack is usually sufficient although some do prefer something slightly bigger. Look for features like padded straps, and multiple compartments for easy organisation. If you're hiking longer distances or carrying heavier loads, ensure the backpack has a hip belt to distribute weight evenly and reduce strain on your shoulders.

Layered Clothing: Dressing for Success

Layered Clothing System

- **Outer Layer** — Protects from wind and rain
- **Insulation Layer** — Adds warmth, retains body heat
- **Fleece Layer** — Traps heat, lightweight and breathable
- **Base Layer** — Wicks sweat, keeps skin dry

Dressing in layers is the key to staying comfortable in changing weather conditions. My four-layer system includes a base layer for moisture management, a middle or fleece layer for warmth, an insulation layer for rest time comfort and an outer layer for protection against wind and rain. This system allows you to add or remove layers as needed, ensuring you stay warm without overheating or sweating excessively.

BASE LAYERS: MOISTURE CONTROL

Your base layer sits closest to your skin and should wick sweat away to keep you dry. Look for materials like merino wool or synthetic fabrics. Cotton has no place when hiking, as it retains moisture and can leave you feeling damp and cold.

Base layers come in various weights, so choose one appropriate for the weather conditions. Lately I have become a fan of mesh base layers as they provide warmth as well as breathability preventing moisture build up.

FLEECE LAYER

The fleece layer provides warmth by trapping heat close to your body. Options include fleece jackets or merino shirts. Fleece is lightweight, breathable, and quick drying, making it a popular choice for hikers. Merino is also very warm but can take a little longer to dry if wet.

The Insulation Layer

The insulation layer provides that added layer of warmth when you need it. I love my synthetic and down insulated jackets for this purpose. At rest stops and around camp I always have an insulation layer on once the sun sets. These layers ensure that the heat trapped by your fleece layer doesn't escape.

> When selecting an insulation layer, consider whether synthetic or down insulation is the best choice for your needs.
>
> **Down jackets** are incredibly warm, lightweight, and packable, making them ideal for dry conditions. However, they lose their insulating properties when wet.
>
> **Synthetic insulation**, on the other hand, retains warmth even when damp and dries faster, making it a more reliable option in wet or humid environments.
>
> If you hike in varied conditions, a synthetic jacket might be the better choice, while down is great for cold, dry weather. Many hikers, including myself, use both depending on the season and conditions.

OUTER LAYERS: WEATHER PROTECTION

An outer layer shields you from wind, rain, and snow. Look for jackets with waterproof and breathable materials like Gore-Tex. Waterproof shells are ideal for rainy conditions, while windproof jackets work well in dry, breezy weather. Some jackets combine these features, offering all-around protection.

> Over time, even high-quality waterproof jackets lose their effectiveness as their **Durable Water Repellent (DWR) coating** wears off. If you notice that water no longer beads on the surface and instead soaks into the fabric, it's time to **re-waterproof your jacket**. You can restore its performance using a **spray-on or wash-in DWR treatment**, which helps maintain breathability while keeping you dry. Regular maintenance ensures your jacket remains a reliable barrier against the elements for years to come.

> Many waterproof jackets have traditionally relied on **per- and polyfluoroalkyl substances (PFAS)**, or "forever chemicals," for water resistance, but these are persistent in the environment and raise health concerns. In response, outdoor brands are developing **PFAS-free waterproofing technologies**. When shopping for a jacket, look for **PFC-free** or eco-friendly water-repellent coatings to reduce your environmental footprint.

Hiking Pants and Shorts

Choosing the right pants or shorts is about balancing comfort, protection, and flexibility. Lightweight, quick-drying pants are great for most conditions, while insulated or waterproof pants are better for cold or wet weather. Waterproof pants are especially useful in places like Tasmania, where sudden rain and muddy trails are common. They also provide an extra layer of protection against overgrown vegetation, sharp branches, and scratchy underbrush, making them a great choice for bushwalking. Convertible pants that zip off into shorts offer versatility for changing temperatures, making them a convenient option for unpredictable conditions.

Hats and Gloves

Head and hand protection is vital for temperature regulation. A wide-brimmed hat or cap shields you from the sun during summer hikes, while a warm beanie and gloves are essential for colder weather.

For winter hikes, opt for gloves with good insulation and wind proofing to prevent heat loss.

> As you progress, you may choose to use a glove system, which works similarly to layering clothing. This involves a lightweight liner glove for dexterity, an insulating mid-layer for warmth, and a waterproof outer shell for protection against wind and moisture. A glove system allows you to adjust for different conditions, keeping your hands warm and functional in extreme weather.

Weather-Related Gear Guide

QUICK REFERENCE FOR HIKERS

HOT & DRY (DESERT, SUMMER HIKES)

- Wear lightweight, moisture-wicking clothing (Merino or synthetic).
- A sun hoodie or breathable long-sleeve shirt provides extra UV protection.
- A wide-brim hat, sunglasses, and sunscreen are essential. Avoid cotton—it traps sweat and dries slowly.

COLD & DRY (ALPINE, WINTER HIKING)

- Start with a wool or synthetic thermal base layer.
- Add a fleece or insulated jacket for warmth.
- A windproof and waterproof shell protects against cold gusts.
- Wear an insulated beanie, gloves, and gaiters to retain body heat.

WET & HUMID (RAINFOREST, COASTAL)

- Choose quick-drying synthetic fabrics.
- A lightweight fleece adds warmth, while a breathable waterproof jacket with vents prevents overheating.
- A rain hat, pack cover, and gaiters help keep you dry.

> ### COLD & WET (SNOW, HIGH ALTITUDE)
>
> - A wool or synthetic thermal base layer is crucial.
> - Add a synthetic puffy or fleece mid-layer for insulation.
> - A fully waterproof, seam-sealed outer shell is necessary for staying dry.
> - Waterproof gloves, a neck gaiter, and goggles protect against snow and wind.
>
> **LAYERING TIP:** Always remove layers before sweating and add them before you start feeling cold. Staying dry is key to comfort and safety in any condition.

NAVIGATIONAL TOOLS

Even on well-marked trails, carrying navigational tools is essential. A paper map and compass serve as reliable backups if your phone or GPS device fails.

Learning how to read a topographic map can make a significant difference in your confidence and safety. Navigation apps like Gaia GPS and AllTrails are excellent digital options but should never replace physical tools entirely.

Equally important is knowing how to use these tools effectively. Simply carrying a map and compass won't help if you don't understand how to navigate with them. I dive deeper into these skills on my [YouTube channel](), where I break down navigation techniques step by step. We'll also go into further detail in a future book, covering advanced navigation strategies to help you feel even more confident in the wilderness.

WATER AND HYDRATION SYSTEMS

Staying hydrated is one of the most important aspects of hiking. Hydration systems like water bladders with drinking hoses allow for hands-free sipping, while reusable water bottles are simple and effective. For longer hikes, consider a portable water filter or purification tablets in case you need to refill from natural sources. We are lucky here in Tasmania that water filtration is rarely an issue but elsewhere it is crucial. Do your research in regards to local water quality and whether or not you need to filter before heading out.

FIRST-AID KIT

A first-aid kit is an essential piece of safety gear for any hike. It should include things like snake bite bandages, antiseptic wipes, blister treatments, pain relievers, and any personal medications. Customise your kit based on the length and remoteness of your hike. Compact, pre-assembled kits are a great starting point but ensure they contain the basics you might need for the area you are hiking in.

SUN PROTECTION

Even on cloudy days, UV rays can harm your skin and eyes. Sunscreen with at least SPF 30, sunglasses, and a wide-brimmed hat are non-negotiables. Look for sunglasses with UV protection to safeguard your eyes from prolonged exposure to the sun.

Trekking Poles

Trekking poles provide stability and reduce strain on your joints, especially during steep descents or long climbs. Adjustable poles are versatile and can be tailored to your height and the terrain. They're particularly useful on uneven or slippery surfaces, offering added balance and support.

Emergency Gear

Unexpected situations can arise, even on short hikes. Carry a whistle, a small torch or headlamp with spare batteries, or a charging battery bank if necessary. A space blanket can provide emergency warmth, and a lightweight emergency shelter is a smart addition for more remote tracks. On most remote day walks I have done over the years; I tend to carry at least a small tarp that I can setup in the event of an unexpected overnight stay!

Multi-Use Items

Multi-use items like bandanas or buffs can serve various purposes, from sun protection to wiping sweat or serving as an impromptu sling. A sturdy knife or multi-tool is another versatile item, useful for cutting, repairing, or preparing food.

Personal Items

Don't forget personal items like an ID, a bit of cash, and your phone. While your phone isn't a substitute for a map and compass, it's a valuable tool for photography, navigation apps, and emergencies. Keep it charged and consider carrying a portable power bank for longer hikes.

Packing Smart

Knowing what to pack is one thing; but how you pack is another. Distribute weight evenly in your backpack, keeping heavier items close to your back and lighter items at the top. Use the backpack's compartments to organise your gear, making frequently used items easily accessible.

Quality vs. Budget

It's tempting to go for the cheapest gear when starting out, but investing in quality essentials pays off in the long run. High-quality gear is more durable, performs better, and can save you money by lasting longer.

That said, there are budget-friendly options that offer good value, especially for beginners testing the waters.

Borrowing or Renting Gear

Before making big purchases, borrow or rent gear if you can. Many outdoor retailers, hiking clubs, or even friends may have gear available to lend, allowing you to try different options before committing.

Renting is a great way to test out expensive items like backpacks, sleeping bags, or tents without the upfront cost. It's exactly how I started out—I had to borrow things like a pack and tent for many years when I first got into hiking. It was a great way to learn about different gear options and figure out what features I wanted when I eventually bought my own. I probably owe my uncle Mark a pack, as his Lowe Alpine backpack was my go-to for years in my early hiking days! Thanks, Mark!

Avoid splurging on a full set of gear until you're sure hiking is something you'll stick with. Start with the basics, upgrading gradually as you gain experience and learn what works best for you.

Hiking preferences vary from person to person, and what seems like a must-have for one hiker might not be necessary for you. Taking your time ensures you invest in gear that truly suits your needs, rather than spending money on items that may end up sitting in storage.

Another great way to save money is to **buy second-hand gear**. Many outdoor shops sell used or refurbished equipment at a discount, and websites or local hiking groups often have gear swap events where you can find quality items for much less than retail price. This is a great way to pick up well-tested, durable gear without breaking the bank.

At the end of the day, focus on getting out there and enjoying the experience rather than feeling pressured to have the best or most expensive equipment. The more you hike, the better you'll understand what gear truly makes a difference for you. Start simple, borrow when possible, and invest wisely once you're confident that hiking is something you love and plan to continue.

At the end of the day, focus on getting out there and enjoying the experience rather than feeling pressured to have the best or most expensive equipment. The more you hike, the better you'll understand what gear truly makes a difference for you.

Start simple, borrow when possible, and invest wisely once you're confident that hiking is something you love and plan to continue.

UPGRADING OVER TIME

As you gain experience, you'll learn which gear works best for you. Start with the basics and upgrade gradually. For instance, you might replace a basic backpack with one that offers more comfort and features or swap inexpensive rain gear for a high-quality waterproof jacket as your hikes become more advanced.

In terms of what gear to buy first here is my personal prioritisation of the MAIN GEAR if I was to start now;

1. Footwear
2. Rainwear
    a. Jacket
    b. Overpants
    c. Gaiters
3. Clothing
    a. Thermals
    b. Fleece
    c. Insulation Layer
4. Sleeping Bag/Quilt
    a. And Sleeping pad
5. Tent
6. Backpack
7. Stove
8. And so on...

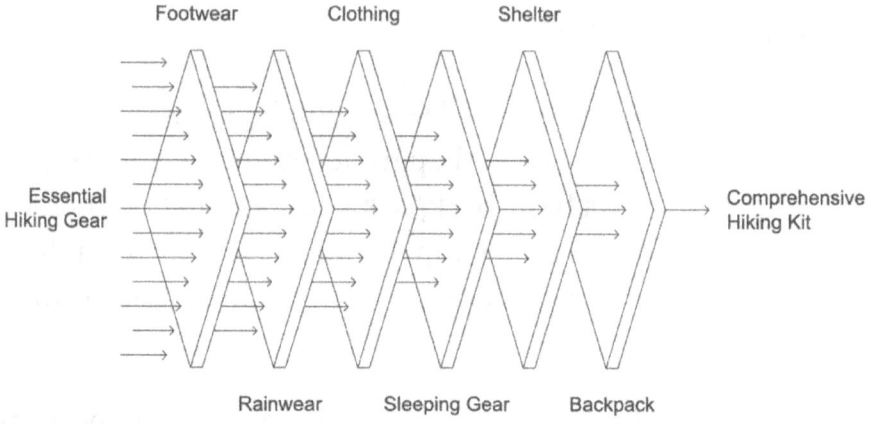

Testing Your Gear

Before heading out on a hike, test your gear at home or on short walks. Practice setting up your backpack, adjusting your layers, and using tools like trekking poles or water filters. Familiarity with your gear ensures that you'll use it effectively when it matters most.

Seasonal Gear Considerations

Different seasons require different gear, and as a beginner, it's best to start hiking in milder conditions rather than jumping straight into winter. Cold weather hiking introduces additional risks like hypothermia, icy trails, and unpredictable weather changes, all of which require experience and specialised equipment.

For winter hikes, you'll need insulated layers, waterproof outerwear, gloves, and proper footwear, along with traction aids like crampons or microspikes for icy terrain. Snowshoes may also be necessary if you're hiking in deep snow. These conditions require extra planning, navigation skills, and awareness of shorter daylight hours.

In contrast, summer hikes often require lighter clothing, extra water, and sun protection. Hot weather increases the risk of dehydration and heat exhaustion, so hydration strategies, electrolyte replenishment, and proper pacing become essential.

Each season presents unique challenges, so adapting your gear accordingly ensures comfort and safety year-round. If you're new to hiking, late spring and early autumn are great seasons to start in Australia, as they offer moderate temperatures and fewer extreme weather conditions.

REFLECTING ON YOUR CHOICES

After each hike, evaluate your gear. What worked well? What didn't? This reflection helps you fine-tune your kit, ensuring it meets your evolving needs as you become a more experienced hiker.

Quick-Reference Day Hike Checklist

(USE THIS LIST TO ENSURE YOU'RE FULLY PREPARED BEFORE HEADING OUT ON A DAY HIKE.)

Also available for download at:

https://www.blog.mowser.com.au/c/gearlist-download

☑ Essentials

- ☐ Daypack (15–30L)
- ☐ Navigation (Map, Compass, GPS/Phone)
- ☐ Headlamp + Spare Batteries
- ☐ Water (2L minimum)
- ☐ Snacks/Energy Food
- ☐ First-Aid Kit
- ☐ Emergency Whistle
- ☐ Sunscreen & Sunglasses
- ☐ Insect Repellent
- ☐ Trekking Poles (Optional but useful)

☑ Clothing & Weather Protection

- ☐ Moisture-Wicking Base Layer
- ☐ Insulating Layer (Fleece/Puffy)*
- ☐ Waterproof/Windproof Jacket
- ☐ Hat (Sun or Beanie for Cold)
- ☐ Gloves (If Needed)
- ☐ Gaiters (For Muddy/Snowy Conditions)*

☑ Miscellaneous & Extras
☐ Multi-Tool or Knife
☐ Camera/Phone + Power Bank
☐ Lightweight Emergency Shelter (Bivy Sack or Space Blanket)
☐ Toilet Kit (Trowel, TP, Ziplock Bag for Waste)

(ITEMS MARKED WITH * ARE OPTIONAL BUT RECOMMENDED DEPENDING ON WEATHER AND TERRAIN.)

Key Takeaways

- Good gear enhances safety, comfort, and enjoyment—you don't need the most expensive items, but investing in reliable essentials makes a difference.
- Footwear is critical—choose hiking shoes or boots suited to the terrain, and always break them in before a big hike.
- Layering is key—a moisture-wicking base layer, an insulating middle layer, and a weatherproof outer layer keep you comfortable in changing conditions.
- Backpacks should be fitted to your needs—for day hikes, 15-30L is usually enough, but ensure it's comfortable and distributes weight properly.
- Navigation tools are essential—carry a map, compass, and a navigation app, but don't rely solely on technology.
- Hydration and nutrition matter—bring enough water and snacks to maintain energy levels, and consider a filtration system for longer hikes.
- Emergency gear can be lifesaving—a whistle, headlamp, first-aid kit, and emergency shelter should always be in your pack.
- Start simple, upgrade over time—borrow or buy second-hand where possible, and gradually invest in better gear as you hike more.
- Test your gear before heading out—practice using your backpack, water filter, and layers to ensure everything works as expected on the trail.

CHAPTER 4

Navigation for Beginners

WHY NAVIGATION SKILLS MATTER

Knowing how to navigate is one of the most essential skills for hikers, no matter how short or easy the trail. While many beginner-friendly trails are well-marked, relying solely on signs or digital tools can lead to trouble if those tools fail or the markers are missing. Good navigation skills not only keep you on track but also give you confidence and independence on the trail. Developing these skills ensures that you can handle unexpected situations, such as missing trail signs, dead batteries, or confusing terrain.

UNDERSTANDING TOPOGRAPHIC MAPS

Maps are your primary tool for understanding the route ahead. A good topographic map shows the path, surrounding terrain, key landmarks, elevation changes, and potential hazards. Familiarising yourself with these features BEFORE you start hiking allows you to mentally map out the journey. Topographic maps provide valuable information about the lay of the land, such as steep inclines or water crossings.

TOPOGRAPHIC MAPS AND CONTOUR LINES

Topographic maps are especially helpful for hikers as they depict the three-dimensional terrain in a two-dimensional format. Contour lines are the key to understanding these maps—they show elevation changes and the shape of the land.

In the following images you will see that lines that are close together indicate steep terrain (as indicated visually by the 3D image), while widely spaced lines mean a gentler slope. Learning to read contour lines helps you anticipate climbs, descents, and potential obstacles like cliffs or ridges.

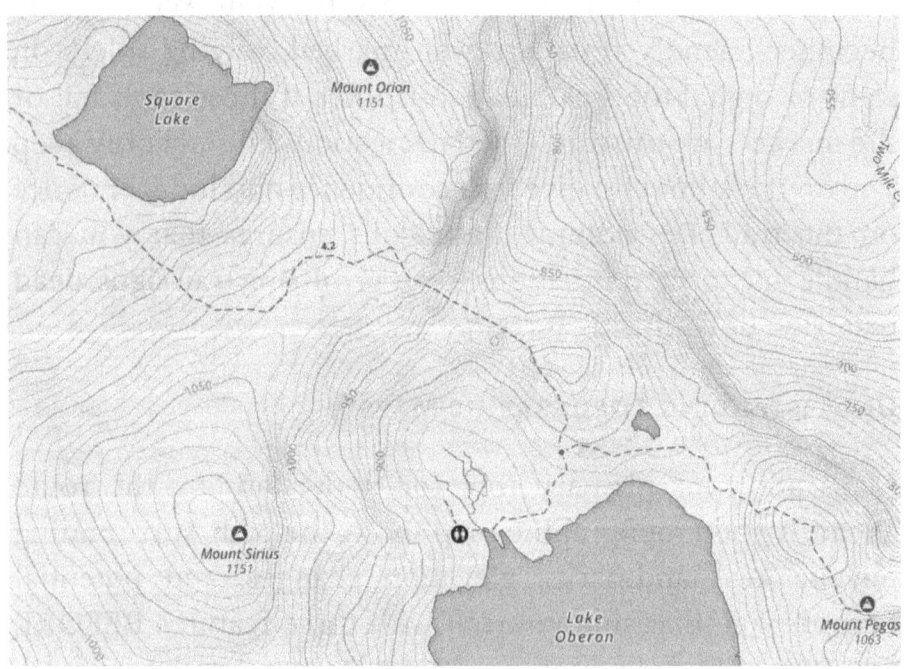

2D Topographic map (from GAIA GPS)

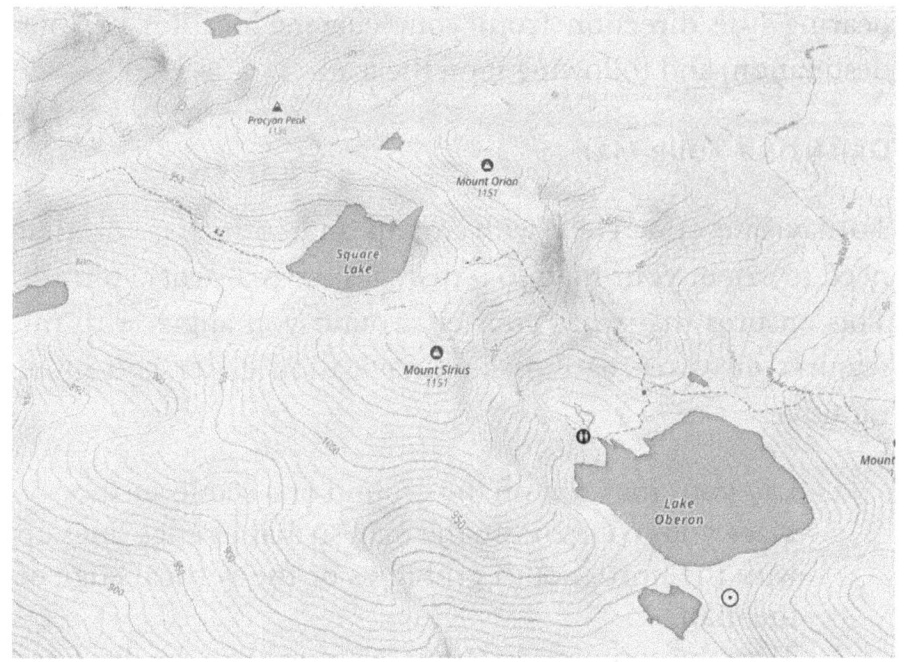

3D Topographic map (from GAIA GPS)

MAP LEGENDS AND SYMBOLS

Every map has a legend explaining its symbols and scale. Familiarising yourself with the legend helps you interpret features like streams, trails, forests, and man-made structures. Pay attention to the scale, which indicates how much ground each unit on the map represents.

USING A COMPASS

A compass is a classic navigation tool that pairs perfectly with a map. While it might seem intimidating at first, learning the basics is straightforward. A compass shows you magnetic north, which helps you orient your map and determine your direction of travel. Practice simple techniques like setting a bearing (the direction from your current location to your destination) and following it on the trail.

Orienting Your Map

To navigate effectively with a map and compass, you first need to orient your map so it matches the real-world terrain. This ensures that what you see around you aligns with the features on your map, making navigation easier and more intuitive.

1. Lay your map flat on the ground or a stable surface.
2. Place your compass on the map so that its edge lines up with the north-south grid lines or the vertical edge of the map.
3. Turn the compass dial until "N" (north) on the dial lines up with the direction of the compass needle.
4. Rotate the entire map (not the compass) until the compass needle is pointing to north on the map.

Now your map is correctly oriented to the landscape, meaning everything in front of you on the ground corresponds to what's in front of you on the map. Take a moment to identify key landmarks, such as mountains, valleys, or water bodies, and match them to their locations on the map. This simple but crucial step helps you visualise your position and navigate with confidence.

Using GPS Devices and Apps

GPS devices, smartphone apps, and watches with inbuilt navigation features have made finding your way on the trail easier than ever. Apps like [AllTrails](#) and [Gaia GPS](#) allow you to download maps, track your location, and plan routes.

However, technology is not foolproof—batteries can die, and signals can be lost, especially in remote areas.

Before heading out, test your navigation apps to ensure they function properly, and try using them in airplane mode to check if they still work offline. Some apps require additional settings to display offline maps correctly. Always carry a paper map and compass as a backup, and make sure your phone or GPS device is fully charged before you start your hike. Taking these extra precautions will help you avoid getting lost if your digital tools fail.

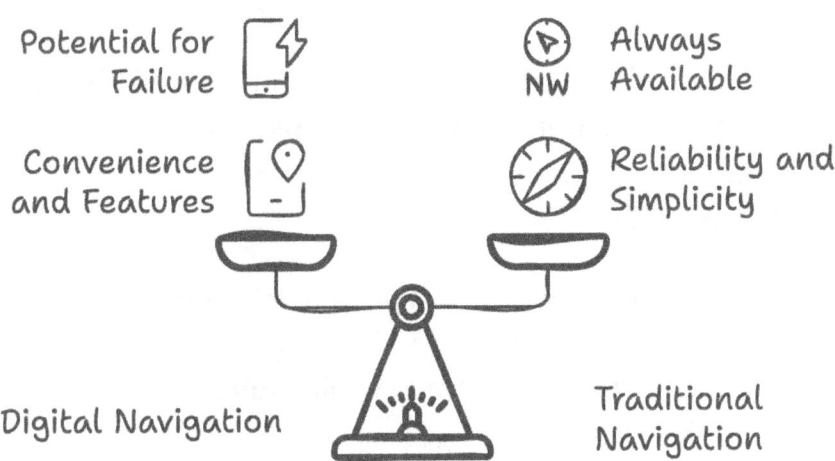

Balance digital convenience with traditional reliability.

Navigating with Landmarks

Using natural landmarks is one of the simplest and most reliable navigation techniques. Features like mountains, rivers, and distinctive trees can help you stay oriented. For example, if a mountain range is consistently to your left, you know you're heading in the correct direction. Combining landmarks with map reading enhances your ability to navigate without constantly relying on tools.

Understanding Trail Markers and Blazes

As we've already discussed, many trails use markers, cairns, tapes or blazes - painted symbols on trees, rocks or posts - to guide hikers. These are especially common on well-maintained trails.

Familiarise yourself with the type of markers used in the area you're hiking, as they can vary. For instance, a single colour might indicate the main trail, while others could signal a change in direction.

Pay attention to these markers but don't rely on them exclusively, as they can sometimes be faded or missing. Especially here in Tasmania, you can sometimes see every type of trail marker on the one walk. Knowing how to read these and follow them correctly is a skill within itself.

Avoiding Common Navigation Mistakes

One of the most common navigation mistakes is assuming that a well-trodden path is the correct one. Trails can intersect or split, leading you off course if you're not paying attention. If many people follow the wrong lead, then an incorrect trail can form. You need to have your wits about you.

Another mistake is neglecting to check your map or app regularly, which can result in wandering too far off your intended route. Always check your position at junctions and take a moment to verify you're on the right path before proceeding.

> Good navigation starts before you even set foot on the track. Study your map or app to plan your route, paying attention to potential challenges like steep climbs or river crossings. Identify key landmarks and stopping points, such as rest areas or scenic lookouts. Knowing what to expect helps you stay prepared and focused during your hike.

Estimating Time and Distance

Understanding how long a hike might take is an important part of planning, but estimating time varies based on terrain, fitness level, weather, and pack weight.

Rather than relying on a fixed formula, it's best to take a flexible approach and allow extra time for breaks, navigation, and unexpected delays.

Elevation gain, rough terrain, and trail conditions all impact your pace. A steep or rocky section will take much longer to traverse than a smooth, flat path.

Instead of trying to predict exact times, focus on tracking your own pace over different hikes. Once you have hiked a few times, you'll get a better idea of how much distance you can comfortably cover within a set time frame, allowing you to plan more accurately.

It's always best to plan conservatively. Allow extra time to reach your destination, set a turnaround time to avoid getting caught out after dark, and be prepared to adjust your plans if needed.

With experience, estimating time and distance will become second nature, making it easier to choose hikes that match your ability and available daylight.

Dealing with Getting Lost

Even with preparation, it's possible to get lost. If you realise you've strayed off course, stop immediately and assess your situation. Look for landmarks and compare them to your map. Retrace your steps to the last known location if it's safe to do so. If you're unable to reorient yourself, stay put and wait for assistance. Carrying a whistle and a PLB (personal locator beacon) and knowing how to signal for help can be lifesaving in such situations.

STAYING CALM AND FOCUSED

Getting lost can be stressful, but panicking only makes the situation worse. Take deep breaths and focus on problem-solving. Check your map, compass, and landmarks carefully. If you're with a group, work together to figure out the best course of action. Remaining calm is key to making sound decisions.

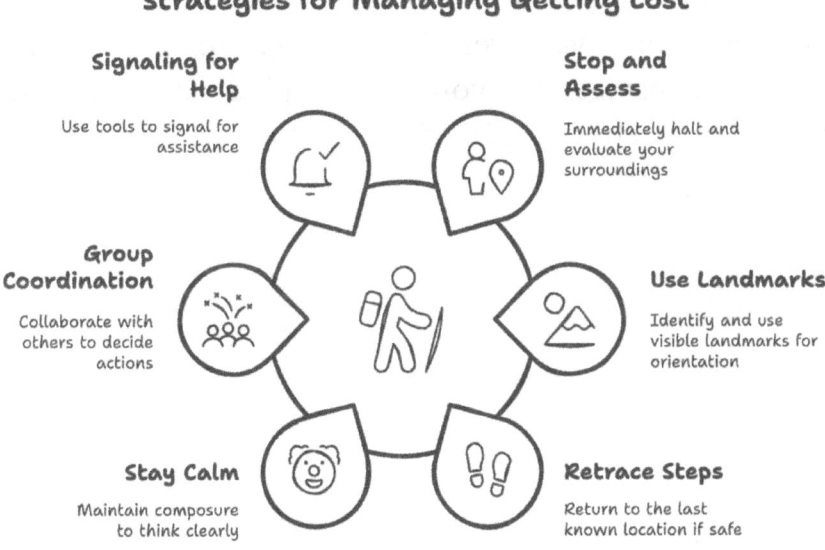

PRACTICING NAVIGATION SKILLS

Navigation is a skill that improves with practice. Start small by using a map and compass on local trails or even in your backyard. Gradually progress to more challenging terrain as your confidence grows. Apps and online tutorials can also help you build your skills. Practicing regularly ensures you're prepared for the unexpected on the trail. Only recently, I have started entering Rogaining races to hone my navigation skills with like-minded people. It is a fantastic way to really improve navigation!

THE CONFIDENCE OF KNOWING YOUR WAY

Mastering basic navigation transforms your hiking experience. It allows you to explore new trails, venture into less-travelled areas, and handle challenges with confidence. As you develop these skills, you'll find that navigation becomes second nature, opening a world of possibilities for your outdoor adventures. By investing time in learning and practicing navigation, you're equipping yourself with the tools to fully enjoy the freedom and beauty of hiking.

Key Takeaways

- **Navigation is a fundamental hiking skill**—relying only on trail markers or digital devices can be risky if they fail or are missing.
- **Topographic maps provide crucial terrain details**—learning to read contour lines helps anticipate elevation changes and key landmarks.
- **A compass is a reliable backup tool**—understanding how to orient a map and follow a bearing ensures you stay on track.
- **GPS apps are useful but not foolproof**—always download maps for offline use and carry a paper map and compass as a backup.
- **Trail markers vary by region**—familiarise yourself with local markers like blazes, cairns, or tapes, but don't rely on them entirely.
- **Regular map checks prevent costly mistakes**—verify your position at junctions and avoid assuming well-trodden paths are the correct route.
- **Estimating time and distance improves with experience**—allow extra time for elevation, rough terrain, and breaks to avoid getting caught out.
- **If lost, stay calm and assess**—stop, check your map and surroundings, retrace your steps if safe, and signal for help if necessary.
- **Navigation skills improve with practice**—start small, use maps on easy trails, and gradually build confidence in more complex terrain.

CHAPTER 5

Planning Your First Hike

THE IMPORTANCE OF PLANNING AHEAD

Planning is one of the most crucial steps for a successful hiking experience, especially for beginners. A well-thought-out plan ensures that you're prepared for the trail, the weather, and potential challenges. It reduces the likelihood of getting lost or overwhelmed and gives you the confidence to enjoy your hike. Proper planning also helps you stay safe, as it accounts for emergencies and unexpected situations.

DEFINING YOUR GOALS

Start by defining the purpose of your hike. Are you looking to enjoy scenic views, test your endurance, or simply spend time outdoors? Your goals will influence your choice of trail, duration, and required gear. For example, a short, easy trail might be perfect if your goal is relaxation, while a longer, more challenging trail suits those seeking physical fitness or a sense of accomplishment.

Choosing the Right Trail

Selecting the right trail is essential for a positive experience. Beginners should focus on trails that match their fitness level and hiking experience. Look for trails with clear markings, gentle inclines, and manageable distances—generally 3 to 5 kilometres (1.9-3.1 miles) for your first hike. Research trail reviews, difficulty ratings, and features like scenic viewpoints or shaded paths to find one that appeals to you.

Understanding Trail Descriptions

Trail descriptions often include key details like distance, elevation gain, and estimated completion time. Pay close attention to these, as they provide a good sense of the trail's difficulty. Elevation gain indicates how steep the trail is; anything above 300 metres can feel challenging for beginners. Combine this information with trail maps to get a comprehensive understanding of what to expect.

Checking the Weather Forecast

Weather conditions can significantly affect your hike. Rain, extreme heat, or strong winds can make even an easy trail difficult. Always check the weather forecast for the trail area on the day of your hike. If the weather looks unfavourable, consider rescheduling or choosing a different trail. Be prepared for sudden changes by packing a rain jacket or warm layer.

Estimating Your Time

Estimating how long a hike will take helps you plan your day and avoid being on the trail after dark. A general rule of thumb for a beginner is to allow 30 minutes per kilometre on flat terrain, adding extra time for elevation gain—add at least 30 minutes per 300 metres of ascent. Consider breaks, photography stops, and your own pace when calculating your total hiking time. An important note here: hiking times are HIGHLY SUBJECTIVE and are hard to estimate until you get to know your rhythm and pace. Always underestimate your times when starting out.

Packing Smart

Packing the right gear is essential for a comfortable and safe hike. Use a checklist to ensure you don't forget anything important. Key items include water, snacks, a first-aid kit, sunscreen, a map, and a rain jacket. Tailor your packing to the trail and weather conditions and avoid overpacking to keep your backpack light and manageable.

Hydration and Snacks

Staying hydrated is crucial, even on short hikes. Carry enough water based upon your needs. Snacks like trail mix, energy bars, and fruit provide the fuel you need to maintain your energy levels. Avoid heavy meals that might make you sluggish on the trail

Understanding the Trail Map

Before you head out, study the trail map to familiarise yourself with the route, key landmarks, and potential challenges. Identify points where you might take breaks, such as lookouts or rest areas. If the trail has junctions or forks, note these and understand which direction to take. Having a clear mental picture of the trail helps you stay oriented.

Planning for Emergencies

Even on well-maintained trails, emergencies can happen. Pack basic safety items like a whistle, a small flashlight, and a multi- tool. Let someone know your plans, including the trail you're taking and your expected return time. This way, they can alert authorities if you don't return as scheduled.

Getting to the Trailhead

Plan how you'll get to the trailhead. Is there parking available? Are there fees or do you need a parks pass? Do you need to book to walk the trail? If you're relying on public transportation, check schedules to ensure you arrive on time. If the trail is remote, consider carpooling with a friend or joining a local hiking group to simplify logistics. And at the end of the walk - have you planned on how to get home once you arrive at the other end?

Starting Early

Starting your hike early has several advantages. Cooler morning temperatures make hiking more comfortable, andstarting early gives you plenty of daylight to complete the trail. It also allows you to enjoy the trail when it's less crowded, making for a more peaceful experience.

Trail Etiquette

Hiking is a communal activity, and observing trail etiquette ensures everyone has a good time. If you are travelling downhill, give way to uphill hikers, stay on designated paths to protect the environment, and keep noise levels down to respect wildlife and other hikers. If you're hiking with a dog, ensure its leashed and clean up after it.

Taking Breaks

Regular breaks help you stay refreshed and maintain a steady pace. Use breaks to hydrate, eat a snack, and take in the scenery. Short, frequent stops are often better than long ones, as they prevent your muscles from cooling down too much. But, having said that, a longer lunch break on a sunny day is too good to pass up. Enjoy it, savour it.

Managing Your Energy

Pacing yourself is key to enjoying your hike. Start slowly to warm up your muscles and maintain a steady pace throughout. Maintaining a pace suited to your fitness is key. Avoid rushing to complete the trail, as this can lead to exhaustion and injuries. Listen to your body and adjust your speed as needed.

Handling Group Dynamics

If you're hiking with others, communicate clearly about the plan, including the trail, expected pace, and break times. Stick together, especially if someone is less experienced. Hiking as a group adds fun and safety, but it's important to ensure everyone's needs are met.

Respecting Nature

Practice Leave No Trace principles to protect the environment. Carry out all of your rubbish, stay on marked trails, and avoid disturbing plants and wildlife. Respecting nature ensures trails remain beautiful and accessible for future hikers.

Knowing When to Turn Back

Part of good planning is knowing when to turn back. If the weather worsens, someone in your group feels unwell, or the trail becomes too challenging, don't hesitate to cut your hike short. Prioritising safety over completing the trail is always the right decision.

Reviewing Your Hike

After your hike, take time to reflect on the experience. What went well? What could you improve next time? Each hike offers valuable lessons that help you become a more confident and prepared hiker. Use these insights to plan your next adventure with greater ease.

Building Confidence Through Preparation

The more you plan, the more confident you'll feel when you hit the trail. Good planning eliminates uncertainty, allowing you to focus on enjoying the hike. Over time, planning will become second nature, and you'll be ready to tackle more challenging trails with excitement rather than hesitation.

By following these planning steps, your first hike will be a safe and enjoyable experience, setting the foundation for many more adventures to come. With each hike, you'll gain confidence, skills, and a deeper appreciation for the outdoors.

KEY TAKEAWAYS

- **Planning ahead is crucial**—a well-prepared hike reduces risks and ensures a more enjoyable experience.
- **Set clear goals**—choose a trail that aligns with your fitness level, time constraints, and interests.
- **Check trail details carefully**—distance, elevation gain, and estimated time all impact difficulty.
- **Weather can change quickly**—always check the forecast and be prepared for sudden shifts.
- **Estimate your hiking time conservatively**—factor in breaks, elevation, and unexpected delays.
- **Pack smart**—essentials include water, snacks, a map, first-aid kit, and weather-appropriate gear.
- **Familiarise yourself with the trail map**—identify key landmarks, junctions, and turnaround points.
- **Inform someone of your plans**—let a friend or family member know your route and expected return time.
- **Start early when possible**—cooler temperatures and ample daylight make for a better experience.
- **Respect the trail and others**—follow Leave No Trace principles, yield to uphill hikers, and keep noise to a minimum.
- **Listen to your body**—take breaks, pace yourself, and turn back if conditions become unsafe.
- **Reflect on your hike**—each experience helps you refine your skills and prepare better for the next adventure.

CHAPTER 6

Food and Hydration on the Trail

THE IMPORTANCE OF FOOD AND HYDRATION

When hiking, food and water are more than just fuel—they're the key to keeping your energy up, your mind sharp, and your body functioning optimally. Whether you're on a short day-hike or tackling an overnight adventure, properly planning your food and hydration strategy can make or break your experience. This chapter dives into the essentials of trail nutrition and hydration, offering practical tips and easy-to-follow advice to help you stay energised and well-prepared on the trail.

UNDERSTANDING YOUR ENERGY NEEDS

Hiking burns a significant amount of energy, especially on steep or lengthy walks. The number of calories you'll need depends on factors like your weight, the intensity of the hike, and the duration. On average, hikers burn anywhere between 300 and 600 calories per hour however this can vary greatly depending on a persons weight, their metabolism and other factors such as terrain and temperature. Meeting these energy demands requires a thoughtful approach to the food you bring, balancing carbohydrates, proteins, and fats for sustained energy and muscle recovery.

THE ROLE OF CARBOHYDRATES

Carbohydrates are your primary energy source while hiking. They provide quick fuel that your body can easily convert into energy. Include carb-rich foods like granola bars, dried fruit, and whole-grain crackers in your trail snacks. These foods are lightweight, easy to pack, and provide a rapid energy boost when you need it most.

INCORPORATING PROTEIN FOR RECOVERY

Protein plays a vital role in muscle repair and recovery. While it's not a primary energy source during your hike, consuming protein ensures your body has the nutrients it needs to recover after exertion. High-protein snacks like jerky, nuts, or protein bars are excellent options for maintaining muscle health during longer hikes.

DON'T FORGET HEALTHY FATS

Fats provide a slow, steady source of energy, making them perfect for sustained activity. Foods like nut butters, olive oil, cheese, and seeds are calorie-dense and offer the added benefit of being satisfying. Combining fats with carbs and protein in your trail mix, snacks ore meals ensures you're hitting all your nutritional bases.

Hydration Is Non-Negotiable

Staying hydrated is crucial for regulating your body temperature, supporting digestion, and maintaining energy levels. Dehydration can lead to fatigue, cramps, or even heat exhaustion, particularly on hot or strenuous hikes. Always prioritise hydration as part of your trail preparation and execution.

Calculating Water Needs

The amount of water you need depends on factors like the weather, your exertion level, and the length of the hike. Always err on the side of caution and carry more water than you think you'll need.

Recognising Signs of Dehydration

Dehydration can sneak up on you, especially if you're focused on the trail. Symptoms include thirst, dark urine, dizziness, and fatigue. If you notice these signs, stop immediately, find some shade, and hydrate. Ignoring dehydration can lead to more severe issues like heat exhaustion or heatstroke.

The Importance of Electrolytes

When you sweat, your body loses not just water but also electrolytes like sodium, potassium, and magnesium. Replacing these is crucial for maintaining muscle function and preventing cramps. Pack electrolyte tablets, powders, or sports drinks to replenish these vital nutrients during your hike.

Factors Contributing to Energy Management in Hiking

Hydration — Essential for maintaining energy levels and preventing fatigue

Carbohydrates — Provide quick energy for immediate fuel needs

Fats — Offer a slow, steady energy source

Proteins — Aid in muscle repair and recovery

PLANNING YOUR TRAIL MEALS

Your meals should be lightweight, non-perishable, and easy to prepare. For day hikes, snacks are often sufficient, but for longer adventures, you'll need a mix of ready-to-eat items and meals that require minimal preparation. Plan meals based on the duration and intensity of your hike, ensuring you have enough food to stay energised without overpacking.

LIGHTWEIGHT AND CALORIE-DENSE FOODS

Weight is a major consideration when packing food for a hike. Opt for lightweight, calorie-dense options like trail mix, energy bars, and dehydrated meals. These foods pack a lot of nutrition into a small package, reducing the load on your back while keeping you well-fed.

QUICK AND EASY TRAIL SNACKS

Trail snacks should be convenient to eat while walking. Granola bars, dried fruit, nuts, and jerky are excellent choices. These items provide a quick energy boost without requiring you to stop and unpack your gear. Keep them easily accessible in your backpack for on-the-go snacking.

PREPPING FOR DAY HIKES

For shorter hikes, your focus should be on simple, no-prep foods. Pack enough snacks to cover the duration of your hike, plus a little extra in case of delays. Foods like

PREPPING FOR OVERNIGHT HIKES

Overnight hikes require more substantial meal planning. Dehydrated meals, which only need hot water, are a popular option for their convenience and lightweight packaging. Combine these with snacks and breakfast items like oatmeal or instant coffee to cover all your nutritional needs.

PACKING EMERGENCY RATIONS

Even on a well-planned hike, unexpected delays can happen. Always carry a small stash of emergency rations, like energy gels or extra trail mix, in case you're out longer than anticipated. These items should be lightweight, calorie-dense, and have a long shelf life.

STAYING ORGANISED

Organisation is key to an efficient food and hydration system. Use small, resealable bags or containers to portion out snacks and meals. This not only makes packing easier but also allows you to monitor how much food you have left during the hike.

Managing Food Waste

Leave No Trace principles apply to food waste as well. Pack out all wrappers, leftovers, and rubbish to keep the trails pristine. Carry a small Ziplock bag for rubbish and store it in a separate pocket of your backpack to avoid contaminating your other gear.

Filtering Water on the Trail

If you're hiking longer distances or in areas with limited water availability, carrying a water filter or purification tablets is essential. These tools allow you to safely drink from natural water sources like streams or lakes, reducing the amount of water you need to carry

Boiling Water for Safety

Boiling is one of the most reliable ways to purify water on the trail. If you're carrying a portable stove, boiling water for at least one minute kills most pathogens, making it safe to drink. This method is especially useful for cooking or preparing hot drinks during colder hikes.

Balancing Weight and Hydration

Water is heavy, and carrying enough for a long hike can add significant weight to your pack. Balance this by planning your route around reliable water sources and bringing a lightweight filter to refill as needed. This strategy reduces your load while ensuring you stay hydrated.

REHYDRATING AFTER THE HIKE

Post-hike hydration is just as important as staying hydrated on the trail. Drink plenty of water or electrolyte-rich beverages after your hike to replace fluids lost through sweat. This helps prevent fatigue and speeds up recovery.

STAYING HYDRATED IN COLD WEATHER

Hydration is just as crucial in cold weather as it is in hot conditions, though it's often overlooked. Cold air can dehydrate you through respiration, and you may not feel as thirsty in cooler temperatures. Make a conscious effort to drink water regularly, even if you don't feel the need.

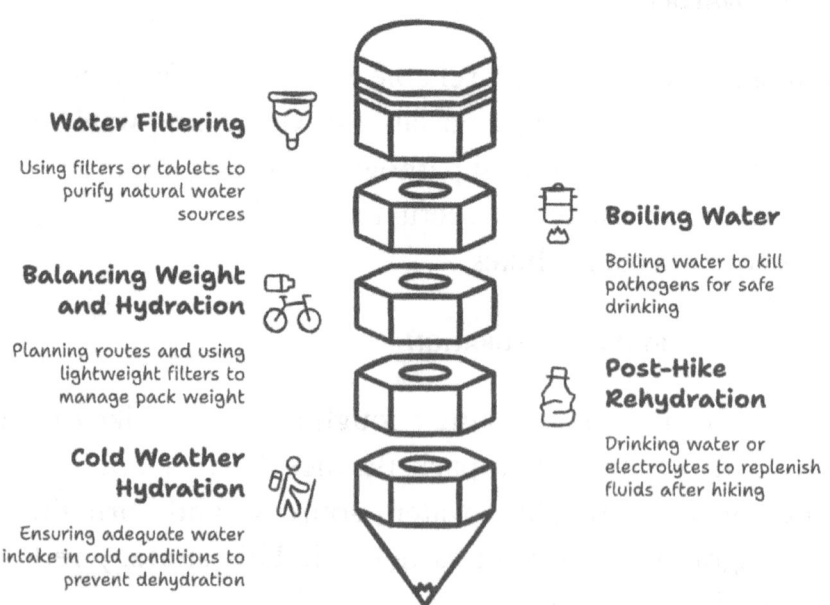

WARM DRINKS FOR COLD HIKES

Warm beverages like tea, coffee, or hot chocolate can provide a psychological and physical boost on chilly hikes. Use a lightweight insulated bottle to keep your drinks warm or pack a portable stove to heat water on the trail.

MANAGING YOUR ENERGY LEVELS

Balancing your energy intake and output is critical for maintaining stamina on the trail. Eat small, frequent snacks rather than large meals to keep your blood sugar stable and avoid energy crashes. Combining carbs, protein, and fats in each snack helps sustain your energy over time.

TAILORING FOOD TO PERSONAL PREFERENCES

Your hiking food should be something you enjoy eating. Familiar, tasty foods are more likely to keep your morale high during challenging sections of the trail. Experiment with different options during practice hikes to find what works best for you.

ACCOMMODATING DIETARY RESTRICTIONS

If you have dietary restrictions, plan your hiking meals accordingly. Many outdoor retailers offer dehydrated meals that cater to specific diets, such as vegetarian, vegan, or gluten- free. Alternatively, you can make your own trail mix or snacks to ensure they meet your needs

Practicing Portion Control

Portion control helps you avoid overpacking food and reduces waste. Calculate how much you'll need based on the duration and intensity of your hike, and pack accordingly. Pre-measuring portions in advance ensures you bring just the right amount.

Testing Your System

Before heading out on a major hike, test your food and hydration system on shorter trips. Practice using your water filter, try out new snacks, and refine your packing strategy. This trial-and-error approach helps you identify what works and what doesn't, ensuring you're fully prepared.

Learning from Experience

Every hike teaches you something new about your food and hydration needs. Reflect on what worked well and what could be improved after each trip. Over time, you'll develop a personalised system that meets your unique preferences and requirements.

Adapting to Different Conditions

Trail food and hydration strategies vary depending on the environment. Hot weather may require more water and salty snacks to replace lost electrolytes, while cold conditions call for higher-calorie meals to generate warmth. Adapt your approach to suit the trail and climate.

KEY TAKEAWAYS

- Fueling properly is essential—carbs provide quick energy, protein aids recovery, and fats offer sustained fuel.
- Hydration is non-negotiable—dehydration can cause fatigue, cramps, and heat exhaustion. Drink regularly.
- Electrolytes matter—replenish sodium, potassium, and magnesium lost through sweat, especially on hot hikes.
- Pack lightweight, calorie-dense foods—trail mix, jerky, dried fruit, and nut butters maximize energy without excess weight.
- Pre-plan your meals—for day hikes, bring snacks; for overnight hikes, consider dehydrated meals for efficiency.
- Emergency rations are a must—carry extra high-energy food in case of delays or unexpected situations.
- Filter or purify water if needed—bring a lightweight filter or purification tablets when refilling from natural sources.
- Balancing weight and hydration is key—carry enough water but use refilling strategies to reduce pack weight.
- Eat small, frequent snacks—this helps maintain stable energy levels and prevents crashes on longer hikes.
- Tailor your food to your preferences—familiar, enjoyable foods boost morale and keep you fueled for the trail.
- Adapt to weather conditions—drink more in heat, increase calories in cold, and adjust based on exertion.
- Learn from experience—refine your food and hydration system with each hike for better efficiency and enjoyment.

CHAPTER 7

Safety Essentials

WHY SAFETY MATTERS IN HIKING

Hiking is an exhilarating way to connect with nature, but the outdoors can be unpredictable. Even on short or well-marked trails, unexpected challenges like sudden weather changes, wildlife encounters, or minor injuries can arise. Safety planning doesn't just prevent problems; it gives you the confidence to handle them if they occur. Understanding and preparing for potential risks ensures that you, and those hiking with you, have a safe and enjoyable experience.

THE TEN ESSENTIALS

The "Ten Essentials" is a checklist for hikers, designed to prepare you for common outdoor emergencies. These items include navigation tools (maps and compass), a headlamp, sun protection, a first-aid kit, a knife or multi-tool, fire-starting materials, extra food and water, extra clothing, a shelter, and a communication device (like a whistle or phone).

Even for short hikes, carrying these essentials can mean the difference between a minor inconvenience and a serious problem.

Navigation Tools

Navigation tools, such as maps, a compass, or GPS devices, help you stay on course and find your way back if you get lost. Learn how to read a map and use a compass before your hike, as these tools don't rely on batteries or signals. While apps like AllTrails are incredibly useful, always have a paper map as a backup in case technology fails.

Proper Footwear

Safety starts with your feet. The right footwear provides stability and protects against slips, falls, and injuries. Choose hiking boots or trail shoes with good grip and ankle support. Make sure they fit well and are broken in before hitting the trail to avoid blisters and discomfort.

First-Aid Kit

A first-aid kit is one of the most critical items in your pack. It should include bandages, antiseptic wipes, adhesive tape, tweezers, pain relievers, blister treatments, and any personal medications. Knowing how to use your kit is just as important as carrying it—consider taking a basic first-aid course to build your skills.

Sun Protection

Exposure to the sun can lead to sunburn, dehydration, and heat exhaustion, even on cool or cloudy days. Pack sunscreen with at least SPF 30, sunglasses with UV protection, and a hat to shield your face and neck. Reapply sunscreen every few hours, especially if you're sweating or in high-altitude areas where UV exposure is stronger.

Staying Hydrated

Dehydration can quickly become dangerous on a hike. Carry enough water for the duration of your trip and consider using a hydration system for easy access. If your hike is longer, bring a water filter or purification tablets so you can safely drink from natural water sources.

Dressing in Layers

As discussed earlier, layering is essential for regulating body temperature and staying comfortable in changing weather. The three-layer system—a moisture-wicking base layer, an insulating middle layer, and a waterproof outer shell—allows you to adjust to varying conditions, whether it's a cold morning start or an unexpected downpour.

Emergency Shelter and Fire Starting

When conditions turn bad or an unexpected overnight stay becomes necessary, having an emergency shelter and a reliable way to start a fire can be lifesaving. **Preparation is key.** A well-thought-out system ensures you stay warm, dry, and visible if rescue is needed.

🔥 QUICK REFERENCE

EMERGENCY SHELTER & FIRE STARTING ESSENTIALS

EMERGENCY SHELTER OPTIONS

- **Bivy sack** – Lightweight, compact, and adds warmth in cold conditions.
- **Space blanket** – Reflects body heat and provides a wind/water barrier.
- **Ultralight tarp** – Versatile shelter that can be rigged between trees.
- **Tent footprint or groundsheet** – Creates a dry base in wet conditions.

FIRE-STARTING ESSENTIALS

- **Waterproof matches** – Store in a sealed container for reliability.
- **Lighter** – A backup ignition source, quick and easy to use.
- **Firesteel (ferro rod)** – Works even when wet and lasts thousands of strikes.
- **Tinder (cotton balls in petroleum jelly, dryer lint, or fire starter cubes)** – Helps ignite a fire quickly in damp conditions.

> ## TIPS FOR QUICK DEPLOYMENT
>
> - **Shelter first.** If you're exposed to the elements, set up your emergency shelter immediately.
> - **Wind protection.** Set up in a windbreak (trees, rocks, or terrain) to minimize heat loss.
> - **Fire placement.** Build a fire near a reflective surface (like a rock face) to trap and radiate heat.
> - **Dry your gear.** If you've been caught in rain, use the fire to dry socks, gloves, or layers.
>
> Having these essentials readily accessible in your pack can **turn a survival situation into a manageable challenge**—and make all the difference when the unexpected happens.

HANDLING WILDLIFE ENCOUNTERS

Wildlife encounters are often a highlight of hiking, but they can also pose risks if animals feel threatened. Research the wildlife in the area you're visiting and learn how to respond to encounters. For example, making noise helps avoid surprising bears, while staying calm and still is key when encountering snakes. Always keep your distance from animals and never feed them.

Communication and Signalling Devices

Carrying a whistle, signal mirror, and a headlamp or torch can be crucial for signalling in an emergency. The international distress signal varies—three short blasts are widely recognized, but in some regions, six blasts repeated at one-minute intervals is also used. If you're hiking in areas without cell service, consider a satellite communication device like a Garmin InReach for SOS alerts and messaging.

Group Safety Dynamics

Hiking with a group adds a layer of safety, but it requires coordination. Agree on a pace that suits everyone, stick together, and check in regularly to ensure no one is struggling. Assign roles, like who carries the first-aid kit or navigation tools, so the group is prepared for emergencies.

Managing Fatigue

Fatigue can increase the risk of accidents, as tired hikers are more likely to trip, fall, or make poor decisions. Listen to your body and take regular breaks to rest, hydrate, and refuel. If you feel overly fatigued, it's safer to cut the hike short than to push through and risk injury.

Recognising Weather Changes

Weather can change rapidly in the outdoors, especially in mountainous areas where conditions shift unexpectedly. Learning to recognise early warning signs—darkening clouds, sudden wind shifts, or a drop in temperature—can make the difference between a controlled response and being caught off guard. Always check the forecast before your hike, but don't rely on it entirely; nature has a way of making its own decisions. Carrying the right gear and staying aware of your surroundings ensures you're ready for whatever the elements throw your way.

> Recently we were on a summer walk in central Tasmania. The day started clear, the sun beating down as we descended the mountain on a hot summer's morning. From our vantage point, we had an uninterrupted view of the surrounding landscape.
>
> In the distance, we spotted something subtle but telling—rain, a distant shifting curtain of grey creeping across the valley opposite us. The wind began to cool, and the air carried the faint scent of moisture. Recognising what was coming, we took a moment to prepare, pulling out our wet weather gear before the rain reached us. When it finally hit, we were ready—dry, warm, and able to continue without interruption.

HANDLING HYPOTHERMIA

Hypothermia occurs when your body loses heat faster than it can produce it, often due to cold, wet, or windy conditions. Symptoms include shivering, confusion, and slurred speech. Prevent hypothermia by staying dry, dressing in layers, and seeking shelter when needed. If someone in your group shows signs of hypothermia, warm them up gradually and get help immediately.

Avoiding Heat-Related Illnesses

Heat exhaustion and heatstroke are serious risks in hot weather. Symptoms include dizziness, headache, and nausea. Prevent these conditions by staying hydrated, wearing light clothing, and taking breaks in the shade. If someone shows signs of heatstroke—confusion, rapid heartbeat, or loss of consciousness—seek emergency help immediately.

Handling Minor Injuries

Minor injuries like cuts, blisters, or scrapes are common on hikes. Clean wounds with antiseptic wipes, apply a bandage, and monitor for signs of infection. For blisters, use moleskin or blister pads to reduce friction and protect the area. Treating small issues promptly prevents them from becoming bigger problems.

Avoiding and Treating Sprains

Sprains are another common hiking injury, often caused by uneven terrain. Wearing proper footwear and using trekking poles can help prevent them. If you or someone in your group suffers a sprain, follow the R.I.C.E. method: Rest, Ice, Compression, and Elevation. Immobilise the affected area if necessary and seek medical attention if the injury is severe.

Staying Alert and Aware

Awareness of your surroundings can prevent many accidents. Stay focused on the trail, especially in challenging sections, and avoid distractions like looking at your phone while walking. Scan the ground for hazards like loose rocks or roots and keep an eye out for trail markers to stay on course.

Letting Someone Know Your Plans

Before heading out, always let a trusted person know your hiking plans. Share details like the trail name, expected start and finish times, and who you're hiking with. If you don't return as planned, this person can alert authorities, significantly improving your chances of being found quickly.

Staying on the Trail

Straying from the marked trail can lead to disorientation, injuries, or damaging the environment. Stick to designated paths and follow trail markers to reduce your risk. If you need to step off the trail for any reason, note your surroundings carefully to ensure you can find your way back.

Practicing Leave No Trace

Safety also includes respecting the environment. Following Leave No Trace principles protects the natural area for future hikers. Pack out all rubbish, avoid picking plants or disturbing wildlife, and minimise your impact on the trail. A clean and safe environment benefits everyone.

Knowing When to Turn Back

Part of staying safe is knowing your limits. If conditions worsen, you're feeling unwell, or the trail is more challenging than expected, don't hesitate to turn back. It's always better to cut a hike short and stay safe than to push on and risk an emergency.

REFLECTING ON SAFETY PRACTICES

After your hike, take time to reflect on your safety practices. Did you feel prepared? What worked well, and what could you improve? Continuous learning ensures you're better equipped for future hikes and helps you build a habit of prioritising safety.

BUILDING CONFIDENCE THROUGH PREPAREDNESS

Safety isn't just about reacting to emergencies—it's about preventing them through preparation and awareness. By carrying the right gear, planning ahead, and learning essential skills, you can hike with confidence and enjoy the outdoors to the fullest. With each hike, your knowledge and preparedness grow, making you a more skilled and self-reliant adventure.

KEY TAKEAWAYS

- **Preparation is key**—unexpected challenges can arise, even on short hikes. Plan ahead and carry essential gear.
- **The Ten Essentials matter**—always pack navigation tools, a headlamp, sun protection, a first-aid kit, a knife, fire-starting materials, extra food and water, extra clothing, a shelter, and a communication device.
- **Navigation is a critical skill**—learn how to use a map and compass, and don't rely solely on GPS apps.
- **Weather can change fast**—check forecasts but stay alert to on-trail signs like darkening clouds or sudden wind shifts.
- **Wildlife encounters require caution**—never approach or feed animals, and know how to respond to potential encounters.
- **Fatigue increases risk**—take regular breaks, stay hydrated, and listen to your body.
- **Know basic first aid**—be prepared to treat minor injuries, blisters, and common hiking ailments.
- **Watch for heat or cold-related illnesses**—heat exhaustion, heatstroke, and hypothermia can be prevented with proper hydration, clothing, and awareness.
- **Let someone know your plans**—sharing your itinerary ensures help can be sent if something goes wrong.
- **Stick to marked trails**—wandering off-trail increases the risk of getting lost and damaging the environment.
- **Recognise when to turn back**—knowing your limits and making smart decisions prevents dangerous situations.
- **Safety builds confidence**—being prepared allows you to hike with greater assurance and enjoy the experience fully.

CHAPTER 8

How to Stay Comfortable Outdoors

COMFORT: THE FOUNDATION OF AN ENJOYABLE HIKE

Staying comfortable while hiking is essential for enjoying your time outdoors. Discomfort can turn even the most beautiful trail into an exhausting ordeal. Whether it's managing the weather, choosing the right clothing, or keeping your energy up, prioritising comfort allows you to focus on the experience rather than on aches, chills, or fatigue. This chapter will guide you through practical tips to ensure a more enjoyable time on the trail.

DRESSING FOR SUCCESS

Clothing plays a significant role in comfort. Layering is the key to adapting to changing temperatures and weather conditions. Start with a moisture-wicking base layer to keep sweat away from your skin, add an insulating middle layer like fleece for warmth, and finish with a waterproof outer layer to protect against wind and rain. This system lets you adjust your layers as needed to maintain a comfortable temperature.

Choosing the Right Fabrics

Not all fabrics are created equal when it comes to hiking. Cotton, for example, absorbs moisture and dries slowly, which can leave you feeling damp and cold. Opt for synthetic materials or merino wool, which wick moisture away from your skin and dry quickly. These materials are also lightweight, making them ideal for packing.

Footwear That Fits

Your feet bear the brunt of every hike, so wearing the right footwear is non-negotiable. Choose hiking boots or trail shoes that fit snugly but don't pinch. Make sure they have adequate arch support and a sole with good traction to prevent slipping. Break in your footwear before your hike to avoid blisters and discomfort. Pair your shoes with moisture-wicking socks to keep your feet dry and reduce the risk of blisters.

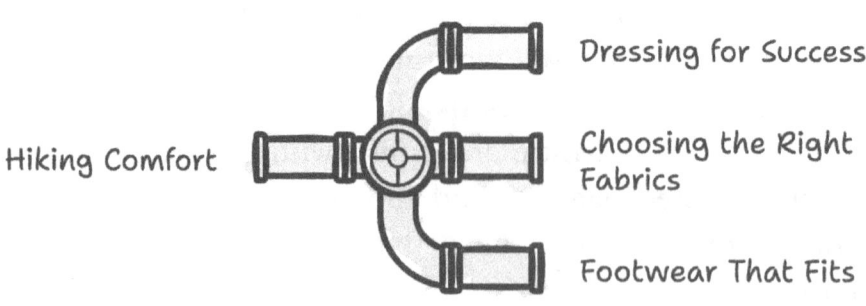

Enhancing Hiking Comfort Through Key Choices

Managing Blisters and Hot Spots

Blisters can turn a pleasant hike into a painful slog. If you feel a hot spot forming—a sign that a blister is developing—stop and address it immediately. Apply moleskin, blister pads, or a layer of medical tape to reduce friction. Keeping your feet dry and wearing well-fitting socks and shoes are your best defences against blisters.

Protecting Against the Elements

Weather can change rapidly, especially in mountainous or exposed areas. Always pack a lightweight rain jacket, even if the forecast looks clear. A wide-brimmed hat or a cap shields you from the sun, while gloves and a beanie provide warmth in colder conditions. Don't underestimate the power of wind; windproof layers can make a significant difference in staying comfortable during breezy conditions.

Staying Warm at Rest Stops

When you stop for a break, your body can cool down quickly, especially in colder weather. To stay comfortable, carry an insulating layer, like a puffy jacket, to put on while you rest. Sitting on a foam pad or a folded jacket can also prevent heat loss to the ground, keeping you warmer and more comfortable.

Managing Temperature on the Move

Hiking generates heat, so you might find yourself sweating even in cooler weather. To avoid overheating, wear breathable clothing and adjust your layers as you hike.

Remove layers before you start sweating heavily, as damp clothes can leave you cold when you stop. Conversely, add layers if you feel a chill to prevent your body from losing too much heat.

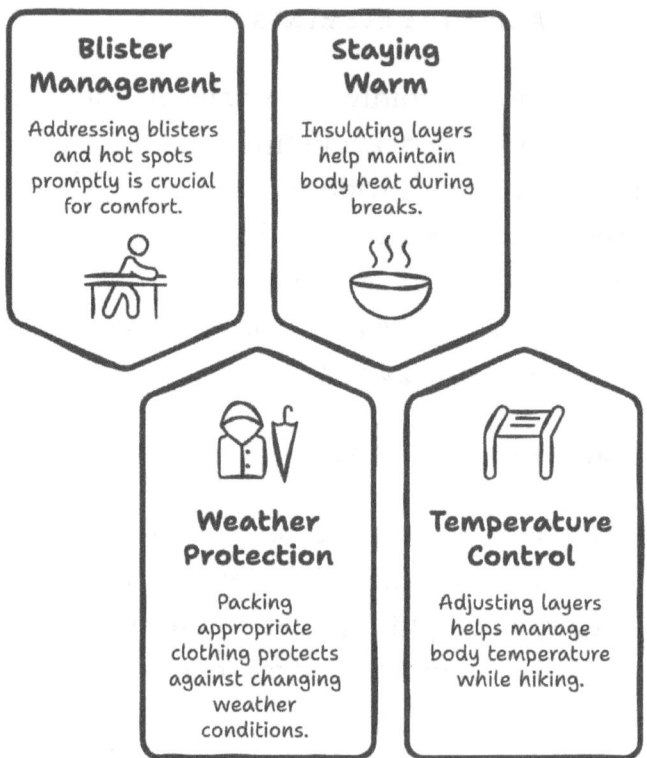

Hiking Comfort and Safety

Blister Management
Addressing blisters and hot spots promptly is crucial for comfort.

Staying Warm
Insulating layers help maintain body heat during breaks.

Weather Protection
Packing appropriate clothing protects against changing weather conditions.

Temperature Control
Adjusting layers helps manage body temperature while hiking.

STAYING HYDRATED FOR COMFORT

Hydration is critical for comfort and performance on the trail. Dehydration can lead to fatigue, cramps, and headaches, making your hike far less enjoyable. Carry enough water for the duration of your hike, and sip regularly rather than waiting until you're thirsty. In hot weather, consider adding electrolytes to your water to replace lost salts and minerals.

Packing Comfort Food

The food you bring on a hike isn't just about nutrition; it's also about morale. Packing snacks you enjoy can give you a psychological boost during challenging sections of the trail. High-calorie, easy-to-eat foods like trail mix, energy bars, and dried fruit are great options. On longer hikes, consider bringing a thermos of soup or hot tea for a comforting treat during rest stops.

Avoiding Chafing and Skin Irritation

Chafing is a common discomfort on hikes, especially during long walks or in humid conditions. It occurs when skin rubs against clothing or other skin. Prevent chafing by wearing moisture-wicking clothing, applying anti-chafe balm to vulnerable areas, and ensuring your backpack fits properly to avoid excessive rubbing on your shoulders or hips.

Maintaining a Balanced Pace

Hiking too quickly can leave you exhausted, while going too slowly might make you feel like you're not making progress. Find a pace that feels sustainable and allows you to enjoy the journey. Use trekking poles to help distribute effort and reduce strain on your knees, especially on steep ascents or descents.

Keeping Your Pack Comfortable

A poorly packed or ill-fitting backpack can cause discomfort and strain over time. Adjust the straps so that the weight is evenly distributed, with the majority resting on your hips rather than your shoulders. Use the backpack's compartments to organise your gear, keeping frequently used items within easy reach.

Taking Regular Breaks

Frequent, short breaks are better than long rests, as they help prevent stiffness and fatigue without causing your body to cool down too much. During breaks, drink water, eat a snack, and stretch your muscles to stay loose and energised. Breaks are also an opportunity to check for any discomfort, such as hot spots on your feet or chafing.

Keeping Morale High

Mental comfort is just as important as physical comfort. Maintaining a positive attitude can help you overcome challenges and enjoy your time outdoors. Celebrate small milestones, like reaching a scenic viewpoint or completing a tough section of the trail. Hiking with friends or engaging in trail activities, like wildlife spotting, can also boost your mood.

Adapting to Different Environments

Different environments present unique challenges for staying comfortable. In desert landscapes, protecting yourself from the sun and carrying extra water are essential. In wet or muddy conditions, waterproof boots and gaiters can keep your feet dry. Understanding the specific demands of the trail you're tackling ensures you pack and dress appropriately.

LEARNING FROM EXPERIENCE

Each hike teaches you something new about what makes you comfortable. Pay attention to what worked well and what didn't, and use that knowledge to refine your approach. Over time, you'll develop a personalised system that keeps you comfortable and happy on the trail, allowing you to fully immerse yourself in the beauty of the outdoors.

PRIORITISING COMFORT FOR LONG-TERM ENJOYMENT

Comfort isn't just about making a single hike more enjoyable—it's about fostering a love for hiking that lasts a lifetime. By prioritising your comfort, you create positive associations with the activity, making it more likely that you'll return to the trails again and again. With the right preparation and mindset, staying comfortable outdoors becomes second nature, allowing you to focus on the joy and freedom of the journey.

KEY TAKEAWAYS

- Layering is key—use moisture-wicking base layers, insulating middle layers, and waterproof outer layers to regulate temperature.
- Choose the right fabrics—avoid cotton; opt for synthetic or merino wool to stay dry and warm.
- Footwear matters—well-fitted hiking boots or shoes prevent blisters and provide support on uneven terrain.
- Manage blisters early—stop and apply moleskin or tape at the first sign of discomfort.
- Be prepared for changing weather—carry a rain jacket, sun protection, and extra layers.
- Adjust layers as you move—remove layers before sweating, add them when cooling down.
- Comfort food boosts morale—pack snacks you enjoy and consider bringing warm drinks for longer hikes.
- Prevent chafing—wear moisture-wicking clothing and apply anti-chafe balm to high-friction areas.
- Find a sustainable pace—avoid burnout by hiking at a steady, comfortable speed.
- Pack smart—distribute weight evenly in your backpack and keep essentials accessible.
- Take regular breaks—short, frequent rests help prevent fatigue and stiffness.
- Keep morale high—celebrate small milestones, enjoy the scenery, and stay positive.
- Adapt to different environments—prepare for heat, cold, mud, or desert conditions accordingly.
- Learn from experience—each hike teaches you what works best for your comfort.

CHAPTER 9

Setting Up for Success on Overnight Hikes

The Unique Challenges of Overnight Hikes

Overnight hikes elevate your outdoor experience, offering the chance to sleep under the stars and wake up surrounded by nature. However, they also bring unique challenges, such as managing gear, cooking, and staying safe through the night. Proper planning and preparation are crucial to ensure your first overnight hike is enjoyable and trouble-free. With the right mindset and knowledge, you can transition from day hiking to overnight adventures with confidence.

Choosing the Right Trail for an Overnight Hike

The first step in planning an overnight hike is choosing the right trail. Beginners should opt for shorter trails with manageable elevation gain, well-marked paths, and designated campsites. Research trails online or consult guidebooks to find options that suit your fitness level and experience. Avoid remote or highly technical trails for your first overnight adventure.

Researching Campsites

Not all campsites are created equal. Some offer amenities like toilets, picnic tables, and water sources, while others are primitive and require more self-sufficiency. Look for designated campsites on your trail map and read reviews to understand what to expect. Ensure camping is permitted in the area and always follow Leave No Trace principles to minimise your impact on the environment.

Packing the Right Gear

Packing for an overnight hike requires careful consideration to balance comfort and weight. A larger backpack, typically 50–65 litres, is essential for carrying extra gear like a tent, sleeping bag, and cooking supplies. Pack only what you need, focusing on lightweight and multi-functional items to reduce your load. Make a checklist to ensure you don't forget essentials like clothing, food, and safety gear.

Choosing a Suitable Tent

Your tent is your primary shelter and one of the most critical pieces of gear for an overnight hike. Look for a lightweight, easy-to-pitch tent that suits the season and conditions of your hike. For mild weather, a three-season tent is sufficient, while four-season tents are designed for colder or more extreme environments. Practice setting up your tent at home to save time and avoid frustration on the trail.

Sleeping Bags and Pad

A good night's sleep is essential for maintaining energy on multi-day hikes. Choose a sleeping bag with a temperature rating appropriate for the conditions you'll encounter. Down sleeping bags are lightweight and compressible but lose insulation when wet, while synthetic bags are heavier but retain warmth even in damp conditions. Pair your bag with an insulated sleeping pad for comfort and to prevent heat loss to the ground.

Dressing for Overnight Comfort

Your clothing choices can make or break your overnight experience. Pack moisture-wicking base layers, an insulating middle layer, and a waterproof outer layer. For sleeping, bring a dedicated set of clean, dry clothes to ensure you stay warm and comfortable through the night. Don't forget warm socks, a hat, and gloves if you're hiking in cooler conditions.

Cooking Gear and Food

Cooking on an overnight hike adds an element of adventure and self-reliance. Invest in a lightweight backpacking stove and cookware set for heating meals and boiling water. Choose dehydrated meals, instant noodles, or other lightweight, easy-to-prepare foods. Bring a small sponge and biodegradable soap for cleaning up after meals.

Managing Water Needs

Water is heavy, so carrying enough for an overnight hike can be challenging. Plan your route around reliable water sources and carry a water filter or purification tablets to treat water from natural sources. Always verify the availability of water on your trail map or through recent reviews, as seasonal changes can affect stream flows.

Organising Your Backpack

Packing your backpack efficiently makes it easier to access gear and keeps the weight balanced. Place heavier items like your tent and food near the centre of your back, and pack lighter items like clothes around them. Keep frequently used items, such as snacks, water, and a rain jacket, in accessible pockets.

Setting Up Camp

Arriving at your campsite with enough daylight to set up is essential. Start by choosing a flat, dry area for your tent, away from potential hazards like falling branches or rising water. Lay out a groundsheet for extra protection and pitch your tent securely using stakes and guy lines. Organise your campsite to keep cooking, sleeping, and waste areas separate.

Building a Comfortable Sleeping Area

Once your tent is set up, prepare your sleeping area. Lay down your sleeping pad and unroll your sleeping bag. Store essential items, like a flashlight, water bottle, and layers of clothing, within easy reach. If you're camping in colder weather, insulate your sleeping area further by layering spare clothes under your sleeping pad.

Managing Food Storage

Proper food storage is critical to prevent wildlife encounters. If you are in North America, you may need to use a bear canister or hang your food in a tree, at least 4 metres off the ground and 2 metres away from the trunk. Never store food or scented items, like toothpaste, inside your tent. If your campsite provides food storage lockers, use them to ensure safety and convenience.

Even in Australia, you do have to sometimes be wary of wildlife and food. In Tasmania, small native animals are infamous for eating holes in tents to items such as food an toothpaste.

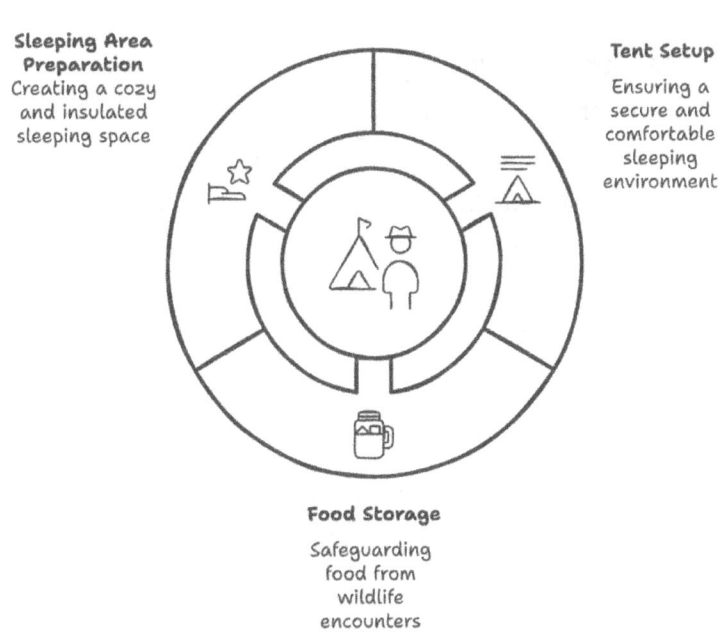

Staying Warm Overnight

Temperature drops can be significant, even in mild weather. To stay warm, eat a calorie-dense meal before bed, wear warm clothing, and use a sleeping bag liner for extra insulation. Close your tent's vents enough to trap heat without causing condensation. If you're still cold, place a hot water bottle inside your sleeping bag for added warmth.

Lighting Your Campsite

A reliable light source is essential for navigating your campsite after dark. Headlamps are ideal because they keep your hands free, but lanterns or compact flashlights are also useful. Bring spare batteries or a backup light to ensure you're not left in the dark.

Hygiene on the Trail

Staying clean on an overnight hike can be challenging, but basic hygiene practices keep you comfortable and healthy. Bring biodegradable soap, a small towel, and hand sanitiser. Use a trowel to dig a cathole for human waste, at least 60 metres from water sources and trails. Pack out all toilet paper and hygiene products to minimise your environmental impact.

Avoiding Insects and Pests

Mosquitoes, ticks, and other pests can make overnight hikes uncomfortable. Carry insect repellent, wear long sleeves and pants, and use a bug net or the mesh of your tent to keep insects at bay. Inspect yourself for ticks regularly, especially in areas where Lyme disease is a concern.

Staying Safe in Bad Weather

Unexpected weather changes are a common challenge on overnight hikes. Pack rain gear, extra layers, and a tarp or emergency shelter for additional protection. If a storm arises, avoid exposed areas like ridges or open fields and seek shelter in lower, forested areas.

Navigating at Night

Moving around at night can be disorienting, especially in unfamiliar terrain. Avoid night hiking unless absolutely necessary and use your headlamp to illuminate the trail ahead. Stick to marked paths and landmarks and proceed cautiously to avoid accidents.

Handling Emergencies

Even with thorough preparation, emergencies can happen. Carry a whistle, first-aid kit, and a communication device like a phone or satellite messenger. Let someone know your itinerary and expected return time before heading out. In case of injury or severe weather, stay calm, assess your options, and act decisively to ensure safety.

Practicing Leave No Trace

Leave No Trace principles are especially important on overnight hikes, as you're spending more time in nature. Pack out all rubbish, minimise campfire impact, and avoid disturbing wildlife or vegetation. Follow campsite rules and guidelines to protect the environment and preserve the area for future hikers.

Managing Group Dynamics

Overnight hikes often involve group settings, which require clear communication and teamwork. Establish roles, such as who sets up the tent or cooks meals, to streamline tasks. Check in with each group member regularly to ensure everyone is comfortable and on the same page.

Winding Down at Camp

Overnight hikes aren't just about the journey; they're also about enjoying the downtime at camp. Take a moment to relax, enjoy the scenery, and reflect on the day. Activities like stargazing, journaling, or sharing stories with fellow hikers make the experience memorable.

Preparing for the Next Day

Before settling in for the night, organise your gear for the next day's hike. Repack your backpack, refill water bottles, and review your map. A little preparation in the evening saves time and reduces stress when you're ready to hit the trail again.

Reflecting on Your Experience

After completing your overnight hike, take time to reflect on what went well and what could be improved. Did you pack the right gear? Were there challenges you didn't anticipate? Use these insights to refine your approach and prepare for future adventures. Each hike builds your skills and confidence, making you a more capable and self-reliant outdoor enthusiast.

By following these guidelines, you'll be well-equipped to tackle your first overnight hike with confidence. With practice and preparation, you'll unlock a new level of hiking experiences, deepening your connection to nature and creating memories that last a lifetime.

Quick-Reference Overnight Hiking Checklist

(USE THIS LIST TO ENSURE YOU'RE FULLY PREPARED BEFORE HEADING OUT ON A MULTI-DAY HIKE.)

Also available for download at:
https://www.blog.mowser.com.au/c/gearlist-download

☑ Backpack & Storage
- ☐ Main Pack (50L+)
- ☐ Pack Liner (Dry Bag/Trash Compactor Bag)
- ☐ Day Pack*

☑ Shelter & Sleep System
- ☐ Tent & Fly
- ☐ Tent Poles & Pegs
- ☐ Sleeping Bag (appropriate for conditions)
- ☐ Sleeping Pad
- ☐ Pillow*
- ☐ Tarp/Groundsheet*

☑ Stove & Cooking
- ☐ Stove & Fuel
- ☐ Cooking Pot
- ☐ Spork/Utensils
- ☐ Cup
- ☐ Hydration Pack (Repack or similar)

☑ Food & Water
- ☐ Water Bladder + Bottle

- ☐ Water Purification (Filter or Tablets)
- ☐ Food for ___ Days
- ☐ Electrolytes*

☑ Clothing (Trail & Camp)
- ☐ Base Layers (Top & Bottom)
- ☐ Insulating Layer (Fleece/Puffy)
- ☐ Waterproof Jacket & Pants
- ☐ Hat & Gloves
- ☐ Spare Socks & Underwear
- ☐ Camp Shoes*

☑ Navigation & Safety
- ☐ Compass & Map
- ☐ GPS Device (Garmin InReach/EPIRB)
- ☐ Head Torch + Spare Batteries
- ☐ First-Aid Kit (incl. Snake Bite Kit)

☑ Hygiene & Miscellaneous
- ☐ Toilet Paper & Trowel
- ☐ Sunscreen & Insect Repellent
- ☐ Toothbrush & Toothpaste
- ☐ Small Repair Kit (Duct Tape, Zip Ties, Sewing Kit)

☑ Optional Items
- ☐ Trekking Poles
- ☐ Camera/Phone + Power Bank
- ☐ Camp Chair*

(ITEMS MARKED WITH * ARE OPTIONAL BUT RECOMMENDED DEPENDING ON CONDITIONS AND PERSONAL PREFERENCE.)

Key Takeaways

- Choose the right trail—start with a well-marked, beginner-friendly route with manageable elevation gain.
- Research campsites—know if they have water sources, toilets, or require a permit.
- Select the right tent—ensure it's lightweight, weather-appropriate, and easy to set up.
- Sleep system matters—pair a suitable sleeping bag with an insulated sleeping pad for warmth and comfort.
- Dress smart—bring moisture-wicking base layers, insulation for warmth, and dry clothes for sleeping.
- Plan meals and cooking—use a lightweight stove and pack easy-to-prepare, calorie-dense food.
- Manage water wisely—carry a water filter or purification tablets and plan around water sources.
- Set up camp properly—choose a flat, dry spot away from hazards, and set up before dark.
- Stay warm overnight—eat a warm meal before bed, insulate your sleeping area, and wear layers.
- Use proper lighting—headlamps are best; always bring spare batteries or a backup flashlight.
- Prioritise hygiene—use biodegradable soap, pack out waste, and follow Leave No Trace principles.
- Be ready for insects—wear long sleeves, use repellent, and check for ticks.
- Prepare for bad weather—carry rain gear and adjust plans if conditions worsen.
- Know emergency protocols—carry a whistle, first-aid kit, and a communication device.

CHAPTER 10

Problem-Solving on the Trail

THE IMPORTANCE OF PROBLEM-SOLVING SKILLS

Hiking often brings unexpected challenges. Whether it's dealing with bad weather, getting lost, or managing minor injuries, being able to problem-solve on the trail is a crucial skill for every hiker. These moments can be stressful, but with the right mindset and preparation, they also become opportunities to build resilience and confidence. Problem-solving involves assessing the situation, staying calm, and using the tools and knowledge you have to address the issue.

STAYING CALM UNDER PRESSURE

The first and most important step when something goes wrong is to stay calm. Panicking can cloud your judgment and make it harder to think clearly. Take a moment to stop, breathe, and assess the situation. This pause gives you the mental clarity to prioritise your next steps. Practice mindfulness techniques during low-stakes situations so that you're better prepared to stay calm when challenges arise.

> ### That Time We Lost the Track in Tasmania
>
> In 1999, I was on an expedition deep in a remote part of Tasmania, following a faint track through dense forest late in the day. After some time, we realised the track had disappeared completely beneath us. With daylight fading fast, we made the decision to stop, set up camp, and regain our composure rather than push ahead blindly.
>
> That evening, we studied the map, discussed our options, and planned a strategy for the morning. With a fresh perspective and rested minds, we located the track again after a short walk the next day and continued on without issue. This experience reinforced a crucial lesson—sometimes, stopping and reassessing is the best decision.
>
> Had we kept pushing forward in fading light, we could have ended up in a far worse situation.
>
> ### Key Takeaway
>
> If you lose the trail, don't panic. Sometimes, the smartest move is to stop, rest, and approach the problem with a clear head in the morning.

DEALING WITH NAVIGATION ERRORS

Getting lost is one of the most common challenges on the trail. If you realise you're off-course, stop immediately and assess your surroundings. Compare the landmarks around you to your map or GPS. Retrace your steps to the last point where you were sure of your location and look for trail markers or blazes. If you're unable to find your way, stay put and use signalling devices like a whistle or flashlight to help rescuers locate you.

MANAGING INJURIES

Injuries like sprains, cuts, or blisters can disrupt your hike, but many are manageable with basic first aid. For cuts and scrapes, clean the wound with antiseptic wipes, apply a bandage, and monitor for signs of infection. For blisters, stop as soon as you feel discomfort, cover the area with moleskin or a blister pad, and adjust your footwear to prevent further rubbing. If you or someone in your group suffers a more serious injury, stabilise them as best you can and seek help immediately.

ADDRESSING WEATHER CHANGES

Weather can change rapidly in the outdoors, especially in mountainous areas. Prepare for sudden shifts by packing extra layers, rain gear, and a hat. If a storm arises, seek shelter under trees or in a low-lying area, avoiding exposed ridges or open fields where lightning strikes are more likely. Keep moving gently to stay warm in cold conditions but avoid overexertion to prevent sweating and subsequent cooling.

HANDLING GEAR FAILURES

Gear failures can range from a broken backpack strap to a torn tent or malfunctioning trekking poles. Carry basic repair tools like duct tape, a sewing kit, and zip ties to address minor issues. For example, duct tape can temporarily fix a rip in your jacket or sleeping pad, while zip ties can secure a broken strap until you return to civilisation. Testing your gear before a hike reduces the likelihood of failures in the first place.

Food and Water Challenges

Running out of food or water can quickly become dangerous. Avoid this by planning carefully and packing extra supplies. If you do run low on water, look for natural sources like streams or lakes, and purify the water with a filter or purification tablets before drinking. For food shortages, ration what you have and avoid exerting too much energy to conserve calories.

Wildlife Encounters

Seeing wildlife can be a highlight of any hike, but certain encounters can be risky. Research the wildlife in your hiking area beforehand and know how to respond. For instance, make noise to avoid surprising bears, and slowly back away if you encounter one. For snakes, give them space and never attempt to handle them. Carrying bear spray or a whistle can add an extra layer of safety in areas with large predators.

Responding to Group Dynamics Issues

Hiking with a group can present its own challenges, such as disagreements about pace, route decisions, or fatigue levels. Communicate openly and check in with each other regularly to ensure everyone is on the same page. If someone in the group is struggling, adjust the pace or take extra breaks to keep morale high. Working together fosters a sense of teamwork and helps resolve conflicts before they escalate.

Technology Failures

While technology like GPS devices and smartphones can enhance navigation and safety, they're not foolproof. Batteries can die, devices can malfunction, and signals can be lost in remote areas. Always carry backup navigation tools, like a map and compass, and know how to use them. A portable power bank can also extend the life of your devices on longer hikes.

Handling Fatigue and Motivation Slumps

Hiking can be physically and mentally exhausting, especially on long or challenging trails. If you or someone in your group is struggling, take a break, eat a snack, and hydrate. Use positive reinforcement to keep morale high and break the hike into smaller milestones to make the journey feel more manageable. Sometimes, even a brief pause to enjoy the scenery can reinvigorate your energy and motivation.

Turning Challenges Into Learning Opportunities

Every challenge you face on the trail is a chance to grow and learn. Reflect on what went wrong, how you handled it, and what you could do differently next time. Over time, these experiences will build your confidence and resilience, making you a more capable and self-reliant hiker. Embrace the mindset that problem-solving is a natural part of hiking, and let each challenge add to the richness of your outdoor adventures.

QUICK-REFERENCE GUIDE FOR COMMON TRAIL PROBLEMS

1. STAYING CALM UNDER PRESSURE

- Stop, breathe, assess. Don't panic—take a moment to evaluate the situation clearly.
- Prioritise actions. Identify the most immediate concern (e.g., shelter, navigation, injury).
- Stay positive. A clear, problem-solving mindset increases your chances of success.

2. DEALING WITH NAVIGATION ERRORS

- Stop as soon as you realise you're off-course. Don't wander further.
- Check your map, GPS, and surroundings. Identify landmarks or retrace your steps.
- Mark your last known location. If necessary, stay put and use a whistle or flashlight to signal for help.
- Use strategy over panic. (See story: That Time We Lost the Track in Tasmania for an example of a good decision.)

3. HANDLING INJURIES

- Minor cuts & open blisters: Clean the wound, apply a bandage, and prevent further friction.
- Sprains or twisted ankles: Use the R.I.C.E. method (Rest, Ice, Compression, Elevation).

- Serious injuries: Immobilise the injured area and call for help if possible.

4. WEATHER CHANGES & SHELTERING

- Recognise early warning signs: Sudden wind shifts, dropping temperature, darkening clouds.
- Act quickly: Put on rain gear before it starts pouring or seek shelter from storms.
- Stay dry & warm: Wet clothing can lead to hypothermia, even in mild temperatures.

5. MANAGING FOOD & WATER SHORTAGES

- Ration your supply: Don't wait until you're out of food or water to plan a solution.
- Find natural water sources: Use a filter or purification tablets before drinking.
- Reduce exertion: If food is low, pace yourself to conserve energy.

6. DEALING WITH GEAR FAILURES

- Carry a basic repair kit: Duct tape, zip ties, needle & thread, and multi-tool.
- Use creative solutions: A broken backpack strap can be reinforced with cordage; a torn jacket can be patched with tape.
- Check gear before you hike: Prevention is always better than field repairs.

7. WILDLIFE ENCOUNTERS

- Stay calm & don't run. Sudden movements can provoke animals.
- Make noise to avoid surprising larger animals. (e.g., bears, wild dogs, etc.)
- Keep food sealed & away from camp. Never leave food scraps behind.

8. TECHNOLOGY FAILURES (GPS, PHONE, HEADLAMP)

- Always carry a backup map & compass. Electronics can fail at the worst times.
- Bring extra batteries or a power bank. Your phone or GPS is useless if it's dead.
- Conserve battery life. Keep your device on airplane mode when not in use.

9. NIGHT TIME EMERGENCIES

- Stay put if you're lost after dark. Navigating at night increases the risk of injury.
- Use headlamp & reflective markers. If you must move, take it slow and stay on visible paths.
- Signal for help. Three or six blasts on a whistle, flashing a light, or creating a visible marker can attract attention.

> **10. KNOWING WHEN TO TURN BACK**
>
> - If the situation worsens, don't push forward. Weather, injury, or exhaustion can make turning back the safest choice.
> - Trust your instincts. If something feels off, don't ignore it.
> - The mountain will always be there. Your safety comes first.

Problem-solving isn't just about reacting—it's about **anticipating issues before they become serious.** With the right mindset and preparation, you can handle most challenges that come your way. Every tough situation teaches you something new, making you a more resilient and capable hiker.

KEY TAKEAWAYS

- **Stay calm first**—panic makes problems worse; take a breath and assess the situation logically.
- **Fix navigation errors quickly**—stop, check surroundings, use a map/GPS, and retrace your steps if needed. If lost, stay put and signal for help.
- **Manage injuries on the spot**—clean wounds, stabilize sprains, and use moleskin for blisters before they worsen.
- **Prepare for sudden weather changes**—carry rain gear, extra layers, and seek shelter if storms arise.
- **Fix broken gear with basic tools**—duct tape, zip ties, and a sewing kit can temporarily repair most failures.
- **Avoid running out of food/water**—carry extra, ration if needed, and know how to purify water from natural sources.
- **Know how to handle wildlife**—avoid sudden movements, stay calm, and back away if necessary. Make noise to prevent unwanted encounters.
- **Resolve group tensions early**—communicate, adjust pace when needed, and maintain team morale.
- **Have a backup for technology**—GPS can fail, so always carry and know how to use a paper map and compass.
- **Fight fatigue and motivation slumps**—hydrate, eat, take breaks, and set small goals to stay mentally engaged.
- **Turn challenges into learning opportunities**—every problem solved makes you a stronger, more resilient hiker.

CHAPTER 11

Learning from Mistakes

EMBRACING MISTAKES AS PART OF THE PROCES

Mistakes are an inevitable part of hiking, especially for beginners. While it can be frustrating to realise you've made an error, these moments are invaluable opportunities for growth. Every misstep, whether it's forgetting an essential item or underestimating a trail's difficulty, teaches you something new about preparation, problem-solving, and resilience. Embracing mistakes as part of the learning process is a key mindset for becoming a confident and capable hiker.

THE VALUE OF REFLECTING ON EXPERIENCES

After a hike, take time to reflect on what went well and what didn't. Did you pack the right gear? Did you encounter unexpected challenges? Reflection helps you identify patterns and areas for improvement, making your next hike more enjoyable and less stressful. Writing your observations in a journal can be especially helpful for tracking progress and lessons over time.

> ### I Lost My Tent Poles on the Way to Federation Peak
>
> Some lessons you only need to learn once—and trust me, losing your tent poles on the way to Federation Peak is one of them. This experience (and many like it) shaped how I hike today, and it's why I wrote PATHFINDER: A BEGINNER'S GUIDE TO HIKING SUCCESS—to help others avoid the same mistakes.
>
> It was the year 2000, and I was making my second attempt at Federation Peak—one of Tasmania's most infamous and formidable climbs. The weather was spectacular, spirits were high, and we were making great progress toward our goal. By day three, after an exhausting eight-hour push in brutal heat, we arrived at Stuart Saddle—a spectacular but exposed campsite with jaw-dropping views. It was the perfect place to recover from the day's grind.
>
> Then, out of nowhere, I turned to see my hiking buddy sitting with his head in his hands.
>
> **"What's wrong?"** I asked.
>
> His response hit me like a ton of bricks: **"I don't have the tent poles."**
>
> In a place where shelter isn't just about comfort but survival, this was not the kind of mistake you want to

make. The area itself is a stark reminder of the dangers of Tasmania's wilderness—named after John Stuart, who perished here in 1956. Suddenly, the stunning views felt a lot less inviting.

We realised the poles must have slipped from my friend's pack at some point during the day's hike. It was now early evening, and exhaustion was setting in fast. My mate decided to retrace our steps for an hour, hoping to find them before dark. Meanwhile, I set about improvising a shelter, rigging up the tent using rope and guy lines.

We made it through the night, thanks to the calm conditions—but it was far from comfortable. The next morning, we made the tough call to backtrack our entire previous day, a brutal decision that cost us our Federation Peak attempt. After hours of retracing our route, we found the poles near the very start of the previous day's walk—a gut-punch of a moment that sealed the fate of this trip.

A few months later, we returned and finally summited Federation Peak. But that experience changed how I approach hiking forever.

Now, every trip I take is guided by the hard-earned lessons from that night—lessons about preparation, gear checks, adaptability, and decision-making that I still use today. Some mistakes you only need to make once, but the key is learning from them so they don't happen again.

Common Packing Mistakes and How to Avoid Them

One of the most frequent mistakes beginners make is overpacking or under packing. Carrying too much gear can lead to unnecessary fatigue, while forgetting essentials like water or a first-aid kit can be dangerous. To avoid these issues, create a packing checklist and stick to it. As you gain experience, refine your list based on what you use during hikes.

The Danger of Ignoring Weather Conditions

Underestimating the weather is another common mistake. Sudden storms, unexpected temperature drops, or intense heat can catch hikers off guard, leading to discomfort or even serious risks like hypothermia or heat exhaustion. Always check the weather forecast before your hike and pack extra layers or rain gear to prepare for changing conditions.

Misjudging Trail Difficulty

Beginners often choose trails that are too challenging for their fitness level or experience. This can result in exhaustion, frustration, or injury. Research trail descriptions carefully, paying attention to factors like distance, elevation gain, and terrain. Start with easier trails and gradually work your way up to more challenging ones as your confidence and stamina grow.

Navigation Errors and Their Lessons

Getting lost on a hike can be both frightening and humbling. Navigation mistakes often occur due to overreliance on technology, neglecting to check the map, or misinterpreting trail markers. The solution is to carry multiple navigation tools—like a map, compass, and GPS—and practice using them before heading out. Regularly checking your position on the map as you hike can prevent minor errors from turning into major detours.

The Role of Communication in Group Hikes

Poor communication in a group hike can lead to misunderstandings, separation, or unmet expectations. For instance, failing to agree on the pace or turnaround time might cause conflicts. Before setting out, discuss the plan with your group, including the route, rest breaks, and contingency plans. Open communication fosters teamwork and ensures everyone enjoys the experience.

Overexertion and Pacing Mistakes

It's easy to get caught up in the excitement of a hike and push yourself too hard. Overexertion can lead to fatigue, dehydration, or injury. Learning to pace yourself is crucial. Start at a steady, comfortable speed and take regular breaks to rest, hydrate, and refuel. Using trekking poles can also help distribute the effort and reduce strain on your legs.

Dealing with Minor Injuries

Blisters, scrapes, and minor sprains are common on the trail. The mistake many hikers make is ignoring these issues until they worsen. Treat blisters and hotspots as soon as you notice them to prevent further discomfort. Carry a well-stocked first-aid kit and learn basic wound care to handle minor injuries effectively.

Underestimating Food and Water Needs

Running out of food or water is a mistake that can quickly escalate into a serious problem. Beginners often underestimate how much energy they'll expend or how much water they'll need. Always pack more food and water than you think you'll use, and learn how to purify water from natural sources in case you run out.

Forgetting the Importance of Breaks

Some hikers, especially beginners eager to finish a trail, skip breaks or take them too infrequently. This can lead to fatigue and reduced focus, increasing the risk of mistakes or injuries. Schedule regular breaks to rest, hydrate, and enjoy the scenery. Short, frequent stops are often more effective than fewer, longer ones.

Navigating Gear Malfunctions

Gear failures, such as a broken strap or a leaking water bottle, are frustrating but manageable with the right mindset. Many hikers learn the value of carrying repair tools like duct tape, zip ties, or a sewing kit after experiencing their first gear malfunction. Testing your equipment before a hike reduces the likelihood of these issues.

Mastering Hiking Fundamentals

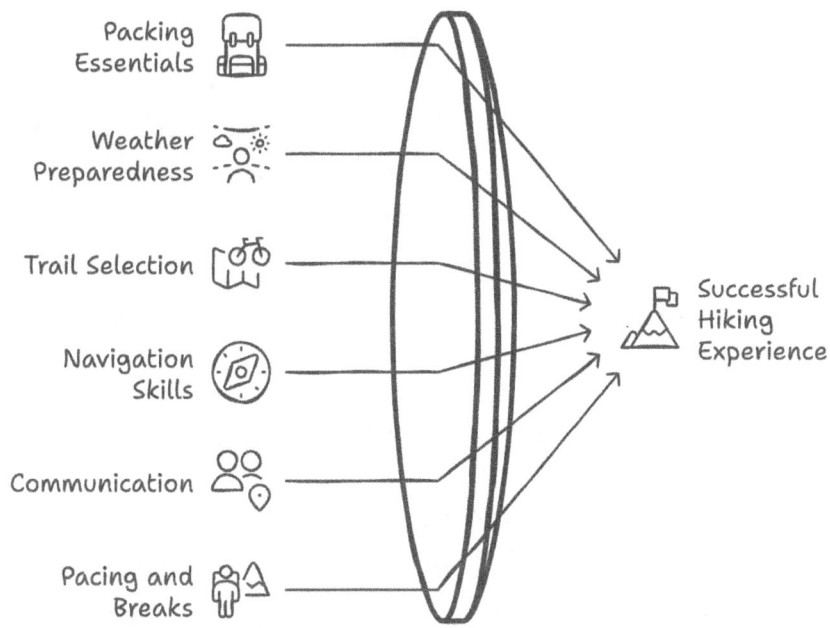

OVERCOMING THE FEAR OF WILDLIFE

Encounters with wildlife can be intimidating, especially for new hikers. However, most animals prefer to avoid humans and will leave you alone if you respect their space. Learn about the wildlife in the area you'll be hiking and how to respond to encounters.

MANAGING OVERCONFIDENCE

Overconfidence can lead hikers to take unnecessary risks, such as attempting a challenging trail without adequate preparation. This often results in mistakes that could have been avoided with a more cautious approach. Respect the trail and your limits, and never underestimate the importance of preparation and research.

Turning Setbacks Into Stories

Mistakes often make for the most memorable hiking stories. Whether it's losing your way and stumbling upon an unexpected viewpoint or improvising when your gear fails, these moments can be opportunities for adventure and creativity. Over time, you'll look back on these experiences with pride and even humour.

Building Confidence Through Experience

Each mistake you overcome builds your confidence and resilience. With every hike, you'll become better at anticipating challenges, solving problems, and adapting to the trail. Over time, the lessons you've learned will make you a more skilled, self-reliant, and prepared hiker.

The Mindset of a Lifelong Learner

Hiking is a lifelong journey of discovery and growth. Even experienced hikers make mistakes, but they view these moments as opportunities to improve. By adopting this mindset, you can turn every challenge into a stepping stone toward becoming a more capable and confident outdoor adventurer. Mistakes aren't setbacks—they're part of the trail to mastery.

KEY TAKEAWAYS

- **Mistakes are essential for growth**—every misstep teaches something valuable about hiking.
- **Reflect after each hike**—review what went well and what could be improved for next time.
- **Avoid common packing mistakes**—overpacking leads to fatigue; underpacking can be dangerous. Use a checklist.
- **Respect the weather**—never underestimate sudden changes. Pack rain gear and extra layers.
- **Choose trails wisely**—start with easier hikes and build up experience before tackling challenging terrain.
- **Improve navigation skills**—don't rely solely on GPS. Carry a map, compass, and know how to use them.
- **Communicate in group hikes**—set expectations for pace, breaks, and emergency plans beforehand.
- **Pace yourself**—hiking too fast leads to exhaustion. Take breaks, hydrate, and use trekking poles if needed.
- **Treat minor injuries early**—don't ignore blisters or scrapes. A well-stocked first-aid kit is a must.
- **Pack enough food and water**—bring extra supplies and learn how to purify water if necessary.
- **Plan for gear failures**—carry duct tape, zip ties, or a repair kit to fix problems on the go.
- **Stay calm around wildlife**—most animals avoid humans. Know how to react to encounters.
- **Don't let overconfidence lead to bad decisions**—respect the trail, your limits, and always be prepared.
- **Turn setbacks into stories**—challenges make for the best adventure memories.
- **Confidence comes with experience**—the more you hike, the better prepared and adaptable you become.

CHAPTER 12

Building Your Confidence and Skills

CONFIDENCE THROUGH PREPARATION

Building confidence as a hiker starts long before you step onto the trail. Proper preparation gives you the knowledge and tools to handle challenges, making you feel secure in your abilities. Research the trail, pack the right gear, and practice basic skills like navigation and first aid. The more prepared you are, the more confident you'll feel when facing the unexpected. Preparation creates a solid foundation that reduces anxiety and lets you focus on enjoying the hike.

START SMALL AND SCALE UP

Confidence grows with experience, and starting small is the best way to build it. Choose short, easy trails that match your fitness level and allow you to practice skills without feeling overwhelmed. Each successful hike, no matter how modest, adds to your confidence. Gradually increase the difficulty and length of your hikes as you become more comfortable with the basics. This step-by-step approach ensures steady progress without unnecessary stress.

Practicing Navigation Skills

One of the most empowering skills for hikers is the ability to navigate confidently. Practice using a map and compass on simple, familiar trails before tackling more challenging ones. Apps like AllTrails or Gaia GPS can supplement your navigation, but knowing how to orient yourself without relying on technology is a valuable skill. With practice, reading topographic maps and recognising landmarks will become second nature, eliminating the fear of getting lost.

Mastering Essential Gear

Becoming familiar with your gear is another key to confidence. Learn how to pack your backpack for balance and accessibility, and practice using essential tools like trekking poles, water filters, and stoves. Setting up your tent or using your navigation tools at home or in a local park can help you feel more capable when it's time to use them in the field. Knowing your equipment inside and out eliminates guesswork and boosts your confidence.

Building Physical Endurance

Hiking is as much a physical activity as it is a mental one, and improving your fitness increases your confidence on the trail. Regular walks, stair climbing, or strength training can prepare your body for the demands of hiking. Start with shorter hikes to build endurance, and over time, tackle more challenging terrain. Feeling strong and capable in your body translates into greater confidence in your ability to handle tougher trails.

Learning from Mistakes

Mistakes are an inevitable part of learning, but they're also one of the best teachers. Reflect on past hikes to identify areas where you can improve, whether it's packing lighter, choosing better footwear, or pacing yourself more effectively. Each mistake overcome adds to your skills and confidence. Embrace these experiences as valuable lessons that make you a better, more prepared hiker.

Hiking with Experienced Companions

Joining more experienced hikers is an excellent way to learn and build confidence. Observing how they navigate trails, manage gear, and handle challenges can teach you valuable tips and techniques. Experienced companions can also provide encouragement and advice, helping you feel more secure as you tackle new experiences. Don't hesitate to ask questions and seek guidance—they were beginners once too.

Setting Achievable Goals

Clear, achievable goals keep you motivated and focused, building confidence as you reach them. For example, your first elevation gain or spend a night outdoors. Celebrate each accomplishment, no matter how small, as a step toward becoming a more skilled and confident hiker.

Developing a Problem-Solving Mindset

Confidence isn't about avoiding challenges—it's about knowing you can handle them. Developing a problem-solving mindset equips you to face obstacles calmly and effectively. Practice assessing situations, prioritising actions, and using the resources at hand to address issues. Whether it's a navigation error or unexpected weather, tackling challenges with a clear head strengthens your confidence in your ability to adapt and thrive.

BUILDING MENTAL RESILIENCE

Hiking can test your mental toughness as much as your physical endurance. Cultivating resilience helps you push through tough moments, like steep climbs or challenging weather. Techniques like positive self-talk, breaking the hike into smaller milestones, and focusing on the rewards—like a scenic view or sense of accomplishment—can keep you motivated. Over time, these mental skills make you more resilient on and off the trail.

SEEKING EDUCATION AND TRAINING

Formal training, like wilderness first aid or navigation courses, can greatly enhance your confidence. These courses provide hands-on experience and knowledge that prepare you for real-life situations. Workshops and online tutorials are also valuable resources for learning specific skills, from packing your backpack efficiently to planning multi-day hikes. Investing in your education builds both competence and confidence.

CELEBRATING YOUR PROGRESS

Acknowledging your growth as a hiker is essential for building confidence. Reflect on how far you've come since your first hike, and take pride in the skills and knowledge you've gained. Sharing your experiences with friends or in hiking communities can reinforce your achievements and inspire others. Confidence thrives when you recognise and celebrate your progress.

Pushing Your Limits Gradually

Challenging yourself to step outside your comfort zone is where real growth happens. Once you've mastered the basics, try tackling a longer hike, a steeper trail, or a new environment like snow or desert hiking. Approach these challenges gradually, ensuring you're prepared and ready for the next step. Successfully pushing your limits builds a sense of accomplishment and reinforces your belief in your abilities.

Becoming a Confident, Lifelong Hiker

Confidence and skill-building are ongoing processes. Each hike adds to your experience and prepares you for new adventures. By combining preparation, practice, and reflection, you'll become a more self-reliant and capable hiker. With time and effort, you'll not only tackle tougher trails with ease but also inspire others to embrace the joy and freedom of hiking. Confidence isn't just about knowing you can handle the trail—it's about feeling empowered to explore the world on your terms.

Key Takeaways

- Preparation builds confidence—research the trail, pack wisely, and practice skills beforehand.
- Start small and progress gradually—begin with easier hikes and increase difficulty as you gain experience.
- Master navigation skills—practice using a map, compass, and GPS so you can navigate with confidence.
- Know your gear—test and practice with equipment before hitting the trail to avoid surprises.
- Improve physical endurance—train with regular walks, stair climbing, and strength exercises.
- Learn from mistakes—reflect on past hikes to refine your approach and avoid repeating errors.
- Hike with experienced people—observe, ask questions, and absorb knowledge from seasoned hikers.
- Set achievable goals—small victories, like completing a longer trail or navigating without GPS, build confidence.
- Adopt a problem-solving mindset—approach challenges calmly and work through them logically.
- Strengthen mental resilience—push through tough moments with positive thinking and small milestones.
- Take courses and training—wilderness first aid, navigation classes, and hiking workshops boost confidence.
- Celebrate progress—acknowledge your improvements and share experiences with others.
- Push limits gradually—once comfortable, challenge yourself with new terrains, weather, or longer hikes.
- Become a lifelong hiker—each experience makes you stronger, more independent, and better prepared for future adventures.

CHAPTER 13

Eco-Friendly Hiking

THE IMPORTANCE OF ECO-FRIENDLY HIKING

As more people discover the joys of hiking, the impact on natural environments grows. Practicing eco-friendly hiking helps preserve the beauty of trails and ensures these spaces remain available for future generations. Being mindful of your actions while hiking reduces harm to ecosystems, protects wildlife, and supports the long-term health of natural areas. Eco-friendly hiking is not just about following rules—it's about fostering a deep respect for the environment and taking responsibility for your role as a visitor.

UNDERSTANDING LEAVE NO TRACE PRINCIPLES

The Leave No Trace (LNT) principles are the foundation of eco-friendly hiking. These seven guidelines—plan ahead, travel and camp on durable surfaces, dispose of waste properly, leave what you find, minimise campfire impact, respect wildlife, and be considerate of others—provide a framework for reducing your environmental footprint. By following these principles, you can hike responsibly and help maintain the integrity of natural spaces.

Planning Ahead to Minimise Impact

Eco-friendly hiking starts with good planning. Research the trail to understand any rules or restrictions, such as designated campsites or fire bans. Check the weather to pack appropriately and avoid unnecessary risks. Planning ahead also means packing reusable or biodegradable items to reduce waste and avoid single-use plastics. Proper preparation minimises the chances of needing to rely on the environment for resources or leaving behind unintended damage.

Staying on the Trail

Sticking to designated trails is one of the simplest ways to protect the environment. Straying from marked paths can damage fragile plants, contribute to soil erosion, and disturb wildlife habitats. Even if a shortcut looks appealing, staying on the trail ensures that your hike has minimal impact on the ecosystem.

Using Durable Surfaces

When camping or taking breaks, choose durable surfaces like rock, sand, or gravel to minimise damage to vegetation. If you're hiking in a grassy or forested area, look for already compacted ground to avoid trampling delicate plants. The goal is to leave the area as untouched as possible, maintaining its natural beauty.

Carrying Out All Rubbish

The principle of "pack it in, pack it out" is central to eco-friendly hiking. Everything you bring onto the trail—wrappers, food scraps, or hygiene products—should be carried back out with you. Bring a small bag specifically for rubbish and dispose of it properly once you return. Even biodegradable items like fruit peels can disrupt local ecosystems and take longer to decompose than you might think.

Reducing Food Waste

Plan your meals carefully to avoid food waste on the trail. Pack only what you need, and use reusable containers for snacks and meals. If you have leftovers, pack them out rather than disposing of them in the wilderness. Properly storing and consuming food not only reduces waste but also helps prevent wildlife from associating humans with food, which can create dangerous situations.

Avoiding Single-Use Plastics

Switching to reusable items is a simple but effective way to reduce waste. Use refillable water bottles, reusable food containers, and cloth napkins instead of single-use plastic alternatives. By making these small changes, you minimise your environmental impact and contribute to the global effort to reduce plastic pollution.

Respecting Wildlife

Hiking offers an incredible opportunity to observe wildlife in its natural habitat, but it's essential to do so responsibly. Keep a safe distance from animals, avoid feeding them, and never disturb their environment. Feeding wildlife can alter their natural behaviours, make them dependent on humans, and even lead to aggressive encounters. Respect their space and allow them to thrive without interference.

Minimising Noise Pollution

Loud noises can disturb both wildlife and other hikers. Speak softly, avoid playing music aloud, and keep group conversations at a moderate volume. Minimising noise pollution creates a more peaceful experience for everyone and helps preserve the natural soundscape of the area.

Choosing Eco-Friendly Gear

Many outdoor brands now offer eco-friendly gear made from recycled or sustainably sourced materials. Look for products with certifications like Bluesign, which ensures environmentally responsible manufacturing. Durable, high-quality gear also reduces waste by lasting longer and requiring fewer replacements.

Using Biodegradable Products

When cleaning up on the trail, use biodegradable soap and products to minimise your impact on the environment. These items break down naturally and reduce the risk of contaminating water sources or harming wildlife. Even with biodegradable items, ensure you use them sparingly and at least 60 metres away from streams or lakes.

Practicing Proper Sanitation

Human waste can be a significant issue on popular trails. Use established restroom facilities when available, or dig a cathole 15–20 centimetres deep and at least 60 metres from water sources to bury waste. Pack out used toilet paper and hygiene products in a sealed bag to ensure they don't pollute the environment.

Minimising Campfire Impact

Campfires are a beloved part of outdoor culture, but they can cause lasting damage to natural areas. Whenever possible, use a portable stove instead of building a fire. If fires are permitted, use established fire sites, keep the fire small, and ensure it's completely extinguished before leaving.

Supporting Conservation Efforts

One of the best ways to practice eco-friendly hiking is by giving back to the environment. Volunteer for trail maintenance projects, donate to conservation organisations, or participate in clean-up events. Supporting these efforts helps preserve natural spaces for future generations and ensures the trails you love remain accessible and well-maintained.

Understanding Ecosystem Sensitivity

Every environment is unique, with its own vulnerabilities and ecological balance. Learn about the area you're hiking in to understand what's at risk and how to minimise your impact. For example, alpine ecosystems are particularly fragile, and even a single footprint can cause lasting damage. By tailoring your practices to the specific environment, you can hike more responsibly.

Avoiding Invasive Species

Invasive species can spread when seeds or organisms hitch a ride on your clothing, shoes, or gear. To prevent this, clean your gear before and after each hike, especially when moving between different regions. Avoid picking plants or carrying natural materials from one location to another to protect local ecosystems.

Practicing Mindful Photography

Capturing beautiful moments on the trail is part of the hiking experience, but it's important to do so without harming the environment. Avoid stepping off the trail or disturbing wildlife to get the perfect shot. Use your camera as a way to appreciate the scenery without disrupting it.

Being a Role Model for Others

Eco-friendly hiking isn't just about your actions—it's also about inspiring others to follow suit. Lead by example by practicing Leave No Trace principles and encouraging your hiking companions to do the same. Share tips and experiences with friends, family, and online communities to spread awareness about responsible hiking practices.

Educating Yourself and Others

The more you know about the environment, the better equipped you are to protect it. Read about local ecosystems, attend workshops, or join guided hikes that focus on conservation. Sharing your knowledge with others helps create a community of environmentally conscious hikers who work together to preserve nature.

Advocating for Sustainable Practices

Beyond the trail, support policies and initiatives that promote sustainable outdoor recreation. Advocate for increased funding for parks, stricter regulations on littering, and the protection of endangered habitats. Your voice can make a difference in ensuring the long-term health of natural spaces.

Making Eco-Friendly Hiking a Habit

Eco-friendly hiking isn't just a set of rules—it's a mindset and a lifestyle. Practicing responsible behaviours on every hike reduces your impact and deepens your connection to nature. Over time, these habits become second nature, enriching your experience while preserving the outdoors for future generations.

Key Takeaways

- **Eco-friendly hiking protects nature**—minimising impact preserves trails for future generations.
- **Follow Leave No Trace (LNT) principles**—plan ahead, stay on trails, dispose of waste, and respect wildlife.
- **Stick to marked trails**—avoiding shortcuts prevents erosion and protects fragile ecosystems.
- **Pack out all rubbish**—everything you bring in should leave with you, including food scraps and hygiene items.
- **Reduce food waste**—plan meals carefully, use reusable containers, and avoid overpacking.
- **Avoid single-use plastics**—use refillable water bottles, cloth napkins, and eco-friendly packaging.
- **Respect wildlife**—observe from a distance, don't feed animals, and leave their habitats undisturbed.
- **Choose eco-friendly gear**—opt for sustainable, durable products to reduce waste.
- **Use biodegradable products**—soaps, wipes, and hygiene products should break down naturally.
- **Practice proper sanitation**—bury human waste properly and pack out toilet paper.
- **Limit campfire impact**—use portable stoves instead of fires, and only burn in designated areas if allowed.
- **Support conservation efforts**—volunteer for trail maintenance, donate to environmental groups, and participate in clean-up events.
- **Understand ecosystem sensitivity**—some environments, like alpine meadows, are easily damaged.
- **Set an example for others**—educate fellow hikers on responsible practices and lead by example.

CHAPTER 14

What's Next? Levelling Up Your Hiking Adventures

BUILDING ON YOUR FOUNDATIONS

Completing your first hikes is just the beginning of a lifelong journey. With a strong foundation of basic hiking skills and experiences, you're now ready to explore new challenges and adventures. Leveling up your hiking means stepping beyond familiar trails, deepening your knowledge, and expanding your horizons. Whether you want to tackle more difficult terrain, hike in different climates, or spend multiple days in the wilderness, the next steps are about pushing your limits while staying safe and prepared.

GRADUALLY INCREASING TRAIL DIFFICULTY

As you grow more comfortable with hiking, challenge yourself with trails that have greater distances, steeper elevation gains, or more rugged terrain. Start with moderate hikes that introduce new elements, like rocky paths or stream crossings, and work up to advanced trails with significant climbs or technical sections. These challenges build strength, endurance, and confidence while keeping your hikes exciting and rewarding.

Exploring Different Environments

Broadening your hiking experiences means exploring a variety of landscapes. If you've mainly hiked in forests, try venturing into deserts, alpine regions, or coastal trails. Each environment offers unique challenges and beauty, from navigating sand dunes to traversing snow-covered trails. Research the specific skills and gear needed for these environments, such as snowshoes for winter hiking or extra water for arid conditions, to ensure you're well-prepared.

Learning Advanced Navigation

While beginner hikes often rely on well-marked trails, leveling up may involve navigating less-defined paths or off-trail routes. Improving your map and compass skills, understanding GPS coordinates, and learning to read natural landmarks like ridgelines or water sources can open up a world of possibilities. Advanced navigation skills give you the confidence to explore remote areas and lesser-known trails.

Tackling Multi-Day Hikes

Once you've mastered day hikes, multi-day adventures are a natural progression. These hikes require additional planning, including route mapping, food preparation, and gear for overnight stays. Start with a single overnight hike to practice carrying a heavier pack and setting up camp, then gradually work up to longer trips. Multi-day hikes allow you to immerse yourself in the wilderness and experience the satisfaction of a self-sufficient journey.

Building a Hiking Community

Hiking with others enriches your experience and provides opportunities to learn and grow. Join local hiking clubs or online communities to connect with like-minded adventurers. Experienced hikers can introduce you to new trails, share tips, and inspire you to push your boundaries. Being part of a community also opens doors to group hikes and organised trips that might be difficult to tackle alone.

Developing Wilderness Survival Skills

Leveling up as a hiker means becoming more self-reliant. Advanced survival skills, like building a shelter, foraging for food, or starting a fire in adverse conditions, can be lifesaving in remote areas. Taking a wilderness survival course or reading up on these techniques equips you to handle emergencies confidently, especially on longer or more isolated hikes.

Capturing Your Adventures

As your hikes become more ambitious, documenting your journeys can deepen your connection to the experience. Invest in a good camera or learn smartphone photography techniques to capture stunning landscapes and memorable moments. Keep a hiking journal to track your progress, record lessons learned, and reflect on the growth you've achieved. Sharing your adventures with others can inspire them to explore the outdoors too.

Planning Bucket-List Adventures

Once you've gained confidence and skills, start dreaming big. Create a hiking bucket list filled with trails or destinations you've always wanted to explore. Whether it's trekking to Everest Base Camp, completing the Overland Track in Tasmania, or hiking the Pacific Crest Trail, these ambitious goals give you something to work toward and inspire you to continue growing as a hiker.

Embracing a Lifelong Journey

Hiking is not just a hobby—it's a lifelong journey of discovery, growth, and connection with nature. Leveling up your adventures doesn't mean rushing into extreme challenges but gradually expanding your skills and experiences. Each trail, new landscape, or challenge tackled brings deeper rewards, shaping you into a more resilient and adventurous person. By continuously learning, adapting, and exploring, you ensure that hiking remains a source of joy and inspiration for years to come.

KEY TAKEAWAYS

- **Keep building on your foundation**—once you've mastered the basics, start challenging yourself with new hiking experiences.
- **Gradually increase trail difficulty**—tackle longer distances, steeper inclines, and rougher terrain as your confidence grows.
- **Explore different environments**—hike in deserts, alpine regions, or coastal trails to gain new skills and adapt to varying conditions.
- **Advance your navigation skills**—practice reading maps, using a compass, and navigating unmarked trails to expand your hiking range.
- **Take on multi-day hikes**—start with an overnight trip **before progressing to longer, self-sufficient treks.**
- **Join a hiking community**—connect with experienced hikers for learning, motivation, and shared adventures.
- **Develop wilderness survival skills**—learn essential skills like shelter-building, fire-starting, and emergency preparedness for remote hikes.
- **Capture your experiences**—document your hikes through photography or journaling to track progress and inspire others.
- **Support conservation efforts**—participate in trail maintenance, advocate for environmental protection, and practice responsible hiking.
- **Plan bucket-list adventures**—set ambitious hiking goals.
- **Embrace hiking as a lifelong journey**—continuous learning, adaptation, and exploration keep hiking rewarding and fulfilling.

Conclusion

THE JOURNEY YOU'VE TAKEN

As you close this guide, take a moment to reflect on the journey we've shared. From learning the basics of trail selection to mastering essential gear and building confidence for overnight hikes, you now have the tools to embark on memorable outdoor adventures. This guide wasn't just about hiking—it was about empowering you to step into the natural world with curiosity, preparedness, and a sense of wonder. Every step you take on the trail adds to a lifelong connection with nature, yourself, and the world around you.

HIKING AS A GATEWAY TO DISCOVER

Hiking is more than an activity; it's a gateway to endless discovery. Each trail you explore unveils unique landscapes, from tranquil forests to towering peaks, and offers new challenges to overcome. Along the way, you discover not only the beauty of the outdoors but also the strength and resilience within yourself. Hiking invites you to slow down, breathe deeply, and appreciate the simple joys that nature provides.

The Value of Preparation

One of the key lessons of this guide has been the importance of preparation. Whether it's packing the right gear, checking the weather, or learning navigation skills, preparation is the foundation of a successful hike. Being prepared not only keeps you safe but also allows you to fully enjoy the experience, free from unnecessary stress or distractions. Preparation is an act of respect—for the trail, for nature, and for yourself.

Confidence Built on Experience

With each hike you complete, your confidence grows. The skills you've learned here—choosing appropriate trails, staying comfortable outdoors, solving problems on the trail—will serve as a foundation for continued growth. Mistakes will still happen, but they're no longer setbacks; they're stepping stones. Over time, you'll find yourself tackling more challenging trails, exploring new environments, and inspiring others to join you.

The Power of Connection

Hiking isn't just about solitude; it's also about connection. Trails connect us to the land and its history, to the people we meet along the way, and to ourselves. Whether you're hiking with friends, joining a group, or simply reflecting in the quiet of the wilderness, these moments of connection add depth and meaning to your adventures. The trail becomes a place where bonds are strengthened, stories are shared, and memories are created.

STEWARDSHIP OF NATURE

Hiking teaches us to value and protect the natural world. As you've learned in the chapter on eco-friendly hiking, your actions on the trail have a lasting impact. By following Leave No Trace principles and advocating for conservation, you become a steward of the environment. Your commitment helps ensure that trails remain open and pristine for future generations, preserving the beauty and wonder that make hiking so special.

EMBRACING CHALLENGES AND GROWTH

The challenges you encounter on the trail—steep climbs, unexpected weather, navigation errors—are not obstacles to avoid but opportunities for growth. Each challenge teaches you something new about yourself and what you're capable of achieving. Embracing these moments with an open mind and a willingness to adapt transforms them into some of the most rewarding aspects of hiking.

THE ENDLESS TRAIL AHEAD

Hiking is a journey with no end. Whether you stick to day hikes or work your way toward multi-day treks, there will always be new trails to explore and experiences to embrace. Each hike deepens your connection to the outdoors and renews your sense of adventure. The skills and knowledge you've gained through this guide are only the beginning; the rest of the story is yours to write, one step at a time.

YOUR NEXT ADVENTURE AWAITS

The time has come to put everything you've learned into action. Start small, dream big, and trust in the skills and confidence you've built along the way. Your next adventure is out there waiting for you, whether it's a peaceful forest trail, a challenging mountain ascent, or a quiet lakeside camp. Lace up your boots, pack your bag, and take that first step—the trail is calling, and it's time to answer.

About the Author

Mowser, an experienced hiking guide and outdoor enthusiast, has spent over three decades exploring some of the most breathtaking regions both on track and off in Tasmania and around the world. As a former guide on Tasmania's iconic Overland Track, Mowser combines his wealth of first-hand experience with a passion for helping others discover the joys of hiking.

Mowser is a content creator known for his weekly newsletter, [Mowser's Musings](#) as well as the popular [YouTube channel](#) dedicated to hiking tips, gear reviews, and practical advice for adventurers of all levels. His content is inspired by years of guiding, personal explorations, and a genuine love for the outdoors.

Known for his practical and accessible approach, Mowser's mission is to empower others to step confidently onto the trail and embrace the transformative power of nature.

In addition to his hiking expertise, Mowser is an entrepreneur, pharmacist, and family man who balances his professional ventures with his love for the outdoors. When he's not hiking through Tasmania's wild landscapes, he's likely spending time with his wife and four sons, tinkering with new gear, or planning his next adventure - be it at home or overseas.

Through his work, Mowser aims to inspire readers and viewers to connect with nature, challenge their limits, and cultivate a lifelong love for exploration.

WWW.MOWSER.COM.AU

Acknowledgments

Writing this, my first book (hopefully the first of many) has been a journey of its own, and I could not have completed it without the incredible support of so many people along the way.

To my wife, your encouragement, understanding, and ability to keep everything running smoothly while I constantly wander off into the wilderness (again) made this possible. To my four boys, your boundless energy and curiosity remind me every day why exploring the outdoors is so important.

To my fellow hiking buddies and guides, thank you for sharing your tips, wisdom, and stories over the years. Your insights and camaraderie have enriched my life in countless ways.

A special thanks to my parents and grandparents for nurturing my love of nature and adventure from an early age. You've instilled in me a deep appreciation for the outdoors that continues to grow.

To the incredible hiking community—whether online, on the track, or through my YouTube channel and Newsletter—thank you for sharing your enthusiasm and feedback. Your passion for the outdoors inspires me to keep creating and sharing.

Lastly, I'd like to acknowledge the pristine beauty of Tasmania and its trails, which have shaped so much of my perspective on hiking. May they remain as wild and breathtaking for generations to come.

www.ingramcontent.com/pod-product-compliance
Lightning Source LLC
Chambersburg PA
CBHW071005160426
43193CB00012B/1919